PAPERS ON
THE ETHNOLOGY & ARCHAEOLOGY
OF THE MALAY PENINSULA

PLATE I

A NEGRITO AT HOME, PENINSULAR SIAM

PAPERS

on the

ETHNOLOGY & ARCHAEOLOGY

of the

MALAY PENINSULA

by

IVOR H. N. EVANS, M.A.

CAMBRIDGE

AT THE UNIVERSITY PRESS

1927

CAMBRIDGE UNIVERSITY PRESS
Cambridge, New York, Melbourne, Madrid, Cape Town,
Singapore, São Paulo, Delhi, Tokyo, Mexico City

Cambridge University Press
The Edinburgh Building, Cambridge CB2 8RU, UK

Published in the United States of America by Cambridge University Press, New York

www.cambridge.org
Information on this title: www.cambridge.org/9781107600652

First published 1927
First paperback edition 2011

A catalogue record for this publication is available from the British Library

ISBN 978-1-107-60065-2 Paperback

PREFACE

THIS small volume consists of papers on the pagan races of Malaya, on Malay beliefs, on Malay technology, and on some of the antiquities of the Peninsula. The materials for it, with the exception of those contained in certain of the papers on antiquities, have already appeared in the *Journal of the Federated Malay States Museums*, or in the *Journal of the Royal Asiatic Society, Straits (now Malayan) Branch*, but republication in the present form renders my work more accessible. In my former book (*Studies in Religion, Folk-lore and Custom in B.N. Borneo and the Malay Peninsula*) I gave the results, up to the date of its publication, of my researches into folk-lore and kindred subjects among the pagan races and the Malays. The papers in the present work, therefore, which deal with such matters may be regarded as supplementary to my other volume.

The sections on neolithic implements, on the cave dwellers and on early bronze and iron tools are new and represent an important advance in our knowledge of the former inhabitants of the Peninsula.

I have to tender my sincere thanks to both the Government of the Federated Malay States and the Malayan Branch of the Royal Asiatic Society for permission to use material already published, and for the loan of blocks and photographs to provide illustrations.

IVOR H. N. EVANS

TAIPING, FEDERATED MALAY STATES.
May 1st, 1927.

CONTENTS

PART I

PAPERS ON THE PAGAN RACES

PART II

MALAY BELIEFS

PART III

MALAY AND OTHER TECHNOLOGY

PART IV

ARCHAEOLOGY

PLATES

*This plate is available for download from
www.cambridge.org/9781107600652

PART I

PAPERS ON THE PAGAN RACES

I. ON SOME NEGRITOS OF PENINSULAR SIAM

Introduction

BEFORE entering upon the subject of this paper, it is necessary to record my most grateful thanks to His Siamese Majesty's Government for the many courtesies that it extended to me through its officers while I was in Siam. H.R.H. Prince Yugala, Viceroy of the Southern Provinces, was kind enough, not only to instruct his officials to help me, but to allow me to occupy his hunting-box at Na Wongse, and to place a launch at my disposal for a visit to the islands of the Inland Sea. Many officers assisted me in various ways, by allowing me to occupy official Rest-houses, with information and advice, or by sending guides or conveyances, and among those whom I must mention are H.E. Phya Kongkha Taratibhodi, Lord Lieutenant of the Surat Circle; H.E. Phya Trangkahuma Phibala, Governor of Trang and H.E. Phya Rasdanupraditha, Governor of Nakon Sritamarat.

Since Old Patalung (Lampam) was my principal base, I was naturally more in contact with the officials of that Governor-ship than elsewhere, and I owe a deep debt of gratitude to both the Governor, Phra Kanasaya Sunthara, for his unfailing kindness in many ways, and to the Deputy-Governor, Khun Narangka Vangsa, my constant companion in Lampam, who most kindly interpreted for me on my second visit to Chong. It is largely owing to his assistance that I have been able to place on record some details with regard to Negrito beliefs and customs.

A road runs from the west-coast province of Trang to the east-coast province of Patalung, and it is in the foot-hills of the main range, through which the road cuts, that the Negritos are to be found living on either side of the divide.

On April 18th, 1924, I entered Siam from Kantang, the port of Trang, and made my first stop in Negrito country at Chong, a royal park containing a large house and several small bungalows; this being situated on the western (Trang) side of the divide. After a few days' intermittent contact with the Negritos here, I went down to Lampam (Old Patalung), on the Inland Sea, to obtain information with regard to the presence of these people in Patalung Province. I found that the best place to work from was a hunting-box on the Trang-Patalung road (belonging to H.R.H. Prince Yugala, Viceroy of the Southern Provinces) at a place spelt Na Wongse, but pronounced Na Wong.

At Na Wongse the Negritos proved "difficult," and I consequently retraced my steps to Chong, where, by the time I left, I had established myself on very friendly terms with them.

My chief difficulty was the question of interpreters. The Negritos, of course, knew no Malay—except one man who had been south and acquired a few words—though they were conversant with the Trang-Patalung dialect of Siamese. To start with, I attempted to use the services of a Dyak collector, who spoke some Siamese, which he had learnt in the north. On my second visit (to Na Wongse and Chong), however, I had the advantage of the presence of the Deputy-Governor of Patalung, who speaks English fluently, and, had it not been for this great assistance, my results would have been extremely meagre. Even he, being a Bangkok Siamese, had occasionally to fall back upon the help of the local headman, since he was unable to understand all the provincialisms employed by the Negritos; and sometimes also they could not understand him.

Appearance, Dress, Character

The Negritos of Chong appear to be fairly typical examples of their race. They are of low stature, and their skin is dark

—though not black. They are considerably more addicted to clothing than their brethren of Perak—though some groups of the latter live in much more "civilized" neighbourhoods. Both are inveterate beggars, though it is probable that the Negritos of Siam fare better in their mendicancy, as the Siamese acquire merit by charity, while the Malay does not give much away to beggars, unless to brother Mohammedans, when alms-giving becomes a duty. It is, no doubt, to Siamese charity that the clothes, worn by both men and women, must be attributed.

In their habits, too, the Chong group seem to be typically Negrito. They appear to plant nothing and to be continually shifting from place to place, living on the tubers which they dig in the jungle and, to some extent, on "game" procured by the blowpipe; for though the blowpipe is not, it is true, an original Negrito weapon, yet it is known to all, and used by all, or almost all, the Peninsular groups.

Distribution of the Negritos in South Siam

On the evidence of the Chong Negritos, others of their kind exist at Kuan Mai Dam, Yong Setar, Trang; at Khao Nam Tow (also in the Yong Setar ampurship), and Khao Ron, Trang, while there are also said to be many in the Kra-Bi Muang. The presence of the Negritos in the Patani States is, of course, well known. They have been visited and described by Annandale and Robinson.

The Chong people seem occasionally to range as far north as Tung Song, and one man told me that he had even been to Nakon Sri Tamarat to see the famous temple there, the Wat Mahadhatu.

I visited Surashtra Dhani (Surat) in consequence of Warington Smyth's statement that Negritos existed, further north, in Province Chaiya, but the Siamese officials declared that there were none to be found. On my return to Kantang, however, just before sailing for Penang, I met an ex-engine-driver, a Sinhalese, who told me that he had often seen them there, so, for the present, I preserve an open mind in this matter.

Names for the Negritos

The Siamese call the Negritos Ngok, Ngok Pa, Chao Pa or Kuan Pa. The first name is preferable. It means "frizzy." The term Chao Pa, which seems to be about equivalent to "jungle folk," appears occasionally to be used in speaking of jungle-dwelling Siamese, and there is thus some danger of confusion arising if one enquires for Negritos under this name.

The Negritos call themselves Monik—Menik is a common term for themselves among the Perak Negritos (cf. Menik Gul, Menik Lanoh)—while they refer to the Siamese as Homik. The Negritos of Selama, in the Malay States, refer to the Malays as Hemik. (*Studies in Religion, Folk-lore and Custom*, p. 185.)

Cranial Measurements

A small number of cranial measurements were taken, these showing an average cephalic index of 78·8:

Name of Negrito and its meaning	Sex and age	Head length in mm.	Head breadth in mm.	Cephalic index
Mai-Pai (a kind of bamboo)	Male about 30 years old	186	142	76·3
Isan (a kind of tree)	Female about 30 years old	177	140	79·0
Paleng (a kind of tree)	Female about 12 years old	172	134	77·9
Wang Kon (name of a stream)	Female of 35–40	172	138	80·2
Kiad (a kind of tree)	Male of 17–18	175	142	81·1
Klieng (? "smooth"; born in a smooth place at the foot of a mountain)	Male about 18 years old	181	142	78·4

The Negrito Headman

Ai-Klieng, I was told, is the headman of the Negritos at Chong, though I-Rom, a woman, seems to be held in some respect. "Ai" and "I," often prefixed to the names of men and women respectively, are, I was informed, low Siamese, and would be resented if used to persons of decent birth. The

Negritos, however, make use of them without scruple when speaking of themselves.

Dwellings

I paid a visit to a Negrito camp in the neighbourhood of Chong, and found that it consisted of typical Negrito wind-breaks of palm leaves, these being arranged in a continuous row. Five sleeping benches were built at right angles to the shelters, and had fires, or the remains of them, close by.

The only objects to be seen in the dwellings were a single blowpipe and quiver, some Chinese-made saucers and brass pots, and some tubers, used for food.

The people that I visited seem to plant nothing and, they told me, are constantly on the move, staying only a few days in each place. The exhaustion of the easily available supply of aroid tubers accounts for this to a large extent, I believe.

Manufactures

The Negritos manufacture so few articles that I was unable to make any considerable collection of specimens. All that I could obtain comprised two complete blowpipes and a portion of the outer tube of another, three quivers containing darts, a necklace of monkey bones, a tube of poison for the blowpipe darts, a few bamboo jews' harps, a small *Pandanus*-covered basket, and some bamboo fire-making apparatus.

Weapons

The Negritos do not appear to use the bow. I made a model of a bow and arrow, and asked them if they knew the weapon. They said that they did, but that it was Siamese, and called it *chendu*. The pellet-bow, for shooting small birds, is constantly to be seen in the hands of the Chong Siamese.

The two blowpipes are without ornamentation. They are constructed of bamboo, and, as do the bamboo blowpipes of the Malay States, consist of an inner and an outer tube. Both of these are built of two pieces. In the outer, protective tube, the distal section appears to fit into the proximal, but the joint is concealed by a rattan binding, covered with a black, gummy substance. It is not easy to see the join when the inner tube is removed, and the interior of the outer tube viewed from one end. The proximal portion of the outer tube is much the longest. The inner tube is constructed of two joints of bamboo, placed end to end, and with a short retaining and strengthening tube, apparently of the same material, encircling the join. This is attached with the same gummy substance, and strengthened with rattan binding. The gum serves not only to keep the tube in place, but also prevents the escape of air. Both ends of the outer tube are covered with this gum, which probably conceals a rattan binding. The lengths of the two portions of the inner tube are about equal. The blowpipe mouthpiece, attached to the inner tube, is also of black gum, covering a rounded piece of bamboo. It is small and roughly spherical.

The quiver is a large bamboo tube without cover of any kind, and without ornamentation. It consists of a single internode and of one of the adjacent nodes, which forms the bottom of the receptacle. Inside the quiver are a number of dart holders—small tubes of bamboo, each for a single dart. These are kept disposed round the inner circumference of the quiver by a wad of dirty cloth, European or Siamese, rammed tightly down the centre. Above this is vegetable fluff, used as a wad behind the darts when they are placed in the blowpipe. Two cords are attached to the quiver which enable it to be tied to the waist.

The darts are very similar to those in use among the wild tribes of the Malay States. They are rather short and consist of a conical head of palm pith and a slender shaft of palm wood, while they are notched above the poisoned point, so that this may break off in the wound when an animal is struck.

The poison presents the same black, gummy appearance as that usually found on Semang and Sakai dart points. The Negritos told me that poison from a creeper (*dok santieng*), that from a tree (*dok kogeung*), birds' fat and the gall of fowls are the materials of which it is composed. The poison obtained from the tree is almost certainly from *Antiaris toxicaria*, while that from a climber is most likely from a species of *Strychnos*.

The following are the Negrito names for some parts of the blowpipe and its appurtenances:

blowpipe	*balau*
outer tube of blowpipe	*yeok balau*
inner tube of blowpipe	*isik balau*
muzzle of blowpipe ...	*sing balau*
dart-quiver	*maneuk*
cords of dart-quiver ...	*sanai maneuk*
head of dart	*yangkam*
dart, whole of ...	*bila**

* (? A Malay numeral coefficient applied to weapons: *e.g. sa'bilah kĕris* —"one *kĕris*.")

Language

A vocabulary of over one hundred and fifty words is given below. Among these quite a number of Malay terms occur, such as those for rice in the husk, cooked rice, banana, coat, a kind of dagger, stone, lake, sweat, wind, elephant, fish, buffalo, duck, three. It is certainly astonishing that names for wild animals should be taken from Malay, and it scarcely seems possible that the Malays can have borrowed from the Negritos, for the Malay word for fish (*ikan*), for instance, in varying forms, is found through Malaysia and Polynesia.

Where, unless they came up from the south, the Negritos got into long and intimate touch with the Malays, seems a matter for further investigation. At the present day, in the province of Patalung, the Malay population is said to be 40 per cent., but it is nearly all in the neighbourhood of the Inland Sea—far from present-day Negrito haunts. In Trang, too, the Malays are, as far as I know, entirely coastal. The most likely explanation appears to be that the Siamese are comparatively recent arrivals in this part of the Peninsula and that, before them, the Negritos retreated into the hills, and the Malays seaward. Up to quite recent times, the Siamese invasion of Kedah and Kelantan was going on apace.

One of the chief objects of my expedition was to find out
whether any distinct Negrito language existed in the Peninsula. The Negrito dialects of the Malay States can, on a set
form of vocabulary, be distinguished from the Sakai dialects
by means of certain key words. Both have, however, an
intimate relation with the Mon-Khmer group of languages
and it seems that, whatever may have been the case with the
Sakai, and whatever their origin, the original language of the
Negritos has been displaced by one borrowed either directly
from the Sakai, or from some former invaders of the Peninsula
who spoke a tongue belonging to the Mon-Khmer group. It
was of considerable interest, therefore, to find out something
about the language of a Negrito tribe which lives far outside
the—at any rate present—area of Sakai influence.

In the list of words that I give below, wherever I have
been able to detect a similar word in use in the Negrito or
Sakai dialects of the Malay States, and recorded in the comparative vocabulary of Skeat and Blagden's *Pagan Races*,
I have given the reference letter and number. It will be seen,
from the large number of these references, that the Chong
Negritos speak a dialect little dissimilar from those of the
Negritos of Malaya. Where I am not able to give a reference,
it is often due to lack of material in *Pagan Races*. Here, too,
then, in Peninsular Siam, the Negritos speak an "adopted"
language.

Vocabulary of the Dialect of the Trang Negritos

English	Negrito	Ref. comp. vocab. Skeat's *Pagan Races*
abuse	*onyok*	
afraid	*ontung*	F 48
afternoon	*amdhui*	D 19
angry	*taheh-goh*	
ant	*les*	A 104
bamboo	*lobeh*	B 21
banana	*piseng*	(Malay *pisang*)
bark (of tree)	*klep (nyrhuk)*	T 211
bear	*kawap*	B 103
bee	*kung gola*	(? cf. Malay *gula*, sugar)
beetle	*nakus*	

English	Negrito	Ref. comp. vocab. Skeat's *Pagan Races*
beetle, dung	*taheum*	*Studies in Religion*, etc., p. 154
big	*eng*	
bird	*kawau*	B 215
blood	*mahum*	B 249
blowpipe	*balau*	B 261
body	*li*	B 321
bone	*i-ying*	B 336
borrow	*lok-luh*	
boy (probably word for "male" given)	*tongkal*	M 15
branch (the word for leaf has been given)	*holik*	L 32
brother, elder	*? tok* ⎫	*Vide* B 411, 413
brother, younger	*? beh* ⎭	
buffalo	*kerbau*	(Malay *kĕrbau*)
butterfly	*uak*	B 479
cat	*mehau*	(Siamese also)
cheek	*tabok*	C 81
cicada (large)	*norit*	
cigarette (native)	*hileh*	
coat	*bajuk*	(Malay *baju*)
coconut	*tung*	
cook, to	*? tasek*	
cord	*santieng*	
cough	*? chempis*	
crocodile	*chongnuk*	
cry, to	*wok wak*	
cut, to	*cha*	C 296
dagger, a kind of	*badik*	(Malay *badik*)
dark	*hokot*	D 16
die	*? posok*	
dig	*hibai*	
duck	*itek*	(Malay *itek*)
dung	*eg*	D 114
durian	*boicheng*	
ear	*onting*	E 6
earth	*teh*	E 12
eat	*heh-hau*	
egg	*tep*	E 36
elbow	*kanyong*	E 42
elephant	*gayah*	(Malay *gajah*)
evening	*amdhui*	D 19
face	*na hadep*	*Vide* "sole of foot"
father	*eh*	F 45
feather	*? chempis*	
fever	*makok*	? F 84
fire	*os*	F 124
fire-place	*topip*	

English	Negrito	Ref. comp. vocab. Skeat's *Pagan Races*
fish	*ikan*	(Malay *ikan*)
flesh	*sik*	F 170
flower	*wehbem*	
fly (*s*)	*yeh*	? F 199
foot	*chan*	F 220
forehead	*pateuk*	F 228
forest	*kaheup*	F 231
fowl	*manuk*	F 257
frightened	*ontung*	
frog	*pong*	
fruit	*habun*	
ghost	*kemoit*, ? *tomis*	G 18
go, to	*hehwai*	
grave, a	*lop*	
hair	*suk*	H 1
hand	*chas*	H 14
head	*kuie*	H 46
heavy	*konung*	
hide (skin)	*koteuk*	S 236
hill	*moleng*	
hoof	*krokok*	N 3
horn	*balung*	H 126
house	*sangak*	
jews' harp	*yen-yeng*	
knife	*katuk*	
leaf	*holik*	L 32
left	*nyek*	
leg, below knee	*komieng*	
leopard, black	*tagok*	? T 130
mad	*ngau*	
maize	*yagong*	(Malay *jagong*)
mantis, praying	*tarok*	
monkey	*baweich*	(pig-tailed macaque) M 134
monkey	*teiyuk*	(? crab-eating macaque)
monkey (leaf-monkey)	*baseng, ai*	M 148 and M 140
moon	*payong*	
morning	*nak-al*	M 178
morrow, to-	*nak-al*	M 178
mosquito	*agis*	(cf. Malay *agas*, sand-fly) M 184
mouth	*tontut*	M 203
nail	*krokok*	N 3
Negrito	*Monik*	M 24
night	*hokot*	D 16
no	*cho-loi*	
nose	*moh*	N 98
nostril	*honeng moh*	H 107 and N 98
oil	? *lepai*	

English	Negrito	Ref. comp. vocab. Skeat's *Pagan Races*
padi	*padi*	(Malay *padi*)
palm of hand	*tapok chas*	(Malay *tapak*, palm)
pig	*gegau*	P 74
piss, to	*konom, chatet*	
potato	*lepai*	
prawn	*? loksuk*	
rain	*het*	
rat	*kadong*	R 33
rattan	*awih*	R 39
rice, cooked	*onchin*	
rice, unhusked and uncooked	*biras onyas*	(Malay *bĕras*)
right	*tim*	R 128
rope	*santieng*	
run	*kochus*	
sago	*koksok*	
salt	*sigak*	S 15
sarong	*gagit patong*	(cf. Malay *patong*, penis)
scorpion (large)	*sosau*	
scorpion (small)	*nipong*	
sea	*tasik*	(Malay *tasek*, lake, sea)
sharp	*chumak*	
shoulder	*kapen*	S 169
Siamese	*Homik*	M 23
sky	*? kagi*	(probably means thunder)
snake	*jekob*	S 310
sole of foot	*hadep chan*	(? cf. Malay *hadap*, "front")
stomach	*ek*	B 161
stone	*batu*	(Malay *batu*)
sweet	*paloh*	(Malay *pĕluh*)
tail	*hertet*	T 3
take hold	*chep*	C 49
tear, to	*? suka*	
thigh	*boleuk*	T 60
tobacco	*bakau*	(Malay *tĕmbakau*)
tortoise	*kopil*	
turn round	*woh-weh*	
turtle, freshwater	*pawis*	
water	*bateu*	W 30
wax	*sul*	? W 48
wind	*angin*	(Malay *angin*)
woman	*kong*	
yes	*oh*	

Numerals

I attempted to get a list of Negrito numerals. The method that I employed was to give a man several paper "cocked-hats" used for wrapping butterflies, and tell him to put them down one by one, counting aloud as he did so. Here are the results of six counts by three or four different individuals:

(1)	*nai*	*nai*	*nai*	*nai*	*nai*	*mampoh*
(2)	*komam*	*komam*	*komam*	*komam*	*komam*	*komam*
(3)	*fobieh*	*fobieh*	*awah*	*awah*	*awah*	*uibem*
(4)	*awah*	—	*tigak*	*tigak*	*tigak*	*ma chongling*
(5)	*uibem*	—	*uibem*	*mampoh*	*mampoh*	—
(6)	*mampoh*	—	*mampoh*	*uibem*	*uibem*	—
(7)	—	—	*tigak*	*fobieh*	—	—
(8)	—	—	*uibem*	—	—	—

It will thus be seen that "one" is, in five out of six cases, given as *nai*, while "two" is in all cases given as *komam*. "Three," in two cases, is *fobieh*, in three *awah*, and in one *uibem*. In one case "four" is *awah*, while in three instances the Malay word for three (*tiga*) was given, but with a final *k* added to it.

When the Negritos were asked to count in Siamese too, they broke down almost at once.

Religion and Custom

The following notes are set down practically as they came from the Negritos, and this accounts for their somewhat disjointed condition.

The Negrito ancestor-king is named Moltek. He lives in the sky, "as high as thunder." Moltek makes fruits for the Negritos. He is very black. He lives in *met ketok*, the sun.

Four persons went with Moltek (who seems originally to have lived at a (?) legendary place called Tangkipeung) to the sky. They were all males, and their names are Chok-bek, Chok-dam, Kalik and Hum. Moltek chews betel; Chok-bek is a "carpenter" and makes houses in which to sleep; Chok-dam fishes and comes back to food at midday; Kalik makes houses, while Hum sells vegetables(!).

There are two kinds of monkeys, one small, named *teiok*, the other large, the *baweich*. The small kind burnt the Negritos' hair and made it frizzy. Their hair was burnt at a place called Tangkipeung. The *teiok* were angry with the Negritos for digging up all the tubers in the jungle. The *baweich*—there were three of them—were on the side of the

Negritos. "The *baweich* went to the sea, but the *teiok* is still here" (*i.e.* in the hills).

The Negritos are frightened of thunder, frightened that it may "hit them on the head." When there is a thunderstorm they hide their eyes with cloths. Kagi makes thunder. He is black. He makes it like "turning the wheel of a cart."

When a person dies, the Negritos shift their camp. The souls of the dead pass to the west and go up to the sky. The soul climbs up a *nipah*-palm and jumps from the top of it across a stream (? the sea). Kot-bŭt is the name of the dark region in the sky to which the spirits find their way. They go around the heavens calling to their friends, those who have passed up before. They meet them, and beckon to them, but their friends run away. Then they go to look for some women, and find them. The spirit of a dead person (*kemoit*) is, at first, very small, like a thread, but it gets bigger when it goes to the sky. The *kemoit* glows with light, like a firefly. The ghost's face looks like that of the clown in the (Siamese play called) *mendora*. The spirits in Kot-bŭt are said to be happy. They do not eat, but they wear clothes.

[There are some interesting points with regard to the monkey legend that I have not yet recorded. One woman said that her mother had told her that the Negritos had come originally from Langka, when it was burnt. Now Langka is the ancient name for Ceylon and, according to the Ramayana, when Sita, the wife of Rama, was stolen by Ravana, the demon King of Ceylon, she was rescued by Rama, who attacked Ceylon, assisted by Hanuman, the monkey-god, and his swarms of monkey followers. It is sometimes stated by students of Indian mythology that these stories of monkey tribesmen are really references to the aboriginal races of India, whose aid Rama sought. Now the legend of how the Negritos obtained their curly hair is found in the Malay States as well, and is also connected with monkeys, while in Peninsular Siam there is a reference to Langka. An interesting point seems to arise, therefore, as to whether a part of the Ramayana story has not been adopted by the Negritos. The Ramayana, with Hanuman, Sri Rama and Sita (Siti Dewi), is still acted in the shadow-show plays of the Siamese and the Malays of the north of the Peninsula.]

As among the Negritos of Perak, children are named after the river, or kind of tree, near which they are born.

When a man becomes engaged to a girl, he continually presents her with dainties, such as monkeys that he has shot with his blowpipe. The man (nowadays) gives a *tical* (a Siamese silver coin) to the girl's mother and father as a bride-price.

Certain articles of food are said to be tabued, among them the flesh of the buffalo, ox, pig and the domestic fowl. The Negritos told me that, if they ate any of these, they would die.

A Siamese Book on the Patalung Negritos

A book, by his late Siamese Majesty, King Chulalongkorn, published in Bangkok and written in the Siamese language, deals with the Patalung Negritos. This is entitled *Bot Lakara Rieng Ngok Pa*, which, I believe, means "the play of the curly (headed) people," or something very near it. The *lakawn* (*lakara*) is a type of play which is said to take its name from Nakon (Sritamarat), also sometimes known as Ligor. The volume, in addition to a vocabulary and notes on the Negritos' customs, contains such a play, in which are described the adventures of "little Kanang," the Negrito boy whom the King took from the Na Wongse neighbourhood to Bangkok. After the late King's death, I am told, Kanang fell on evil days, and eventually died.

There are several good reproductions from photographs in the volume, one of Kanang freshly caught; a second of the hero's friends and relations with three of the men carrying blowpipes, a third of him in theatrical costume, and a fourth of him in court dress, as a royal page, I believe. The cover bears a picture of Kanang's Negrito instructor in magic, who has vaulted on to the back of a tiger, already wounded in the eye by a poisoned dart, and is about to stab it with a dagger.

II. NOTES ON PAHANG NEGRITOS

In September and October, 1913, while on an expedition to Pahang, I visited certain Negrito groups on the Cheka River, and an account of these people appeared in the *Journal of the F.M.S. Museums* (vol. v, part 2, pp. 193–204). The present paper is supplementary to the former notes. A vocabulary, taken on the Cheka, in 1913, appeared in vol. VI, part 2.

Starting from Kuala Lumpur, by motor car, on May 11th, 1925, I proceeded to Batu Balei, a small Malay settlement on the Benta-Kuantan Road. From this place I went up the Cheka by boat to Lata Lang—normally a day's journey. This village, the scene of my former labours in the *ulu*, was, in 1913, a newly opened Malay settlement. It has now developed considerably.

Finding that there were not many Negritos at Lata Lang —most of them being away collecting *jĕlutong* (a kind of wild rubber from which chewing-gum is made)—I returned to Batu Balei and, from there, went to Jeransang, also on the Benta-Kuantan Road, but some fourteen miles nearer to Benta. Here I met another, though closely related, group of Negritos, and from them I gained most of the information contained in this paper.

Tribal Name

The Negritos of Jeransang, and also those of Cheka, are called Batek by the Malays. The former group term themselves Bateg Hapen, after a local stream which the Malays call Sepan, and the Negritos Hapen.

Fire-making

The Negritos of the Ulu Cheka denied that they know of any methods of making fire other than by means of flint-and-steel, and ordinary matches, purchased from the Chinese. They produced an example of their strike-a-light apparatus.

Weapons

I have given a detailed description of the Cheka blowpipe and dart-quiver in my former paper on these people, and the specimens purchased on the present occasion differ but little from those with which I have already dealt. The only two blowpipes that I obtained both had conical mouthpieces and two-piece inner and outer tubes. I found that the existence of the bow was known, and my Jeransang informant gave me the ordinary Negrito name for the weapon (*loid*), though he had never seen a specimen.

Habitations

I visited two camps, one at Lata Lang, the other near Jeransang. Both of these were typically Negrito, being composed of mere wind-breaks of palm leaves, and each containing, as usual, a sleeping bench and fire. At Kuala Cheka, in 1913, I noted, and recorded (*loc. cit. supra*, p. 194) a more advanced type of dwelling, which was said to have been constructed by the Negritos themselves.

Clothes, and Personal Adornment

I have alluded to the many-coiled rattan girdles (*lapai sĕgak*), and their magical patterns, in another section of this paper. These articles are worn by the women. Another type of girdle is of cord made of the fibre of the sugar palm. The Malays call the tree *Kabong*, and the cord made from the fibre *tali ijok*. One specimen of this kind of girdle was purchased: it consists of many coils and, at one end, other cord, seemingly of banana fibre, has been added. A man's girdle of plaited strands of what the Malays call *akar batu* (a black fungus rhizomorph) was also obtained. Bracelets of *akar batu*, or of brass wire, are fairly commonly to be seen.

The bamboo combs (*kenaid*), used by the women, are clumsy and badly made. They are usually decorated with rudely scratched-in patterns of poor execution. Specimens of bark cloth, very dirty from use as loin-cloths, were seen in the shelters. Both brown bark cloth and white are made, the former probably from the *Tĕrap* (*Artocarpus* sp.), the latter from the Ipoh (*Antiaris toxicaria*).

Face-Painting and Tattooing

I have recorded in my former paper that both face-painting and tattooing are found among the Cheka Negritos. Tattooing was noted on some of the women at Jeransang, this usually consisting of one or two large dark blue spots on the forehead. Face-painting was also to be seen, and I obtained a stamp consisting of a piece of stick divided into sections at one end by making repeated cuts with a knife, these passing from side to side and through the centre. Using this for applying the gummy paint, one lady had covered her thighs with flower-like designs.

Religion and Beliefs

Most of my information under this heading was collected at Jeransang. I suspect that the name Bonsu (a Malay word meaning "youngest born," better *bongsu*), given to the younger brother of the two ancestor-deities, is derived from Sakai sources—for certain Sakai heroes are so called—though the two personages appear to have typically Negrito attributes. Here are the details about them:

Teng and Bonsu, elder and younger brothers, live above the seven layers of the sky. Bonsu looks after fruits and flowers. His fruits fall from above, and his flowers also, and become fruits and flowers on earth. He arranges the fruit evenly on a mat. Teng also looks after fruits and flowers. They are both black, like Negritos, and wear cords crossed on their breasts. If Bonsu were to come down to earth, the whole world would dissolve and become a sea. There is nobody in the seven layers of the sky.

Jawait lives below the clouds and makes thunder. He has a long beard and meets the souls of dead shamans. His wife, Lai-oid, lives under the earth. She makes *talain*[1]. She wears

---

[1] Thunderstorms accompanied by welling up of water from under the earth, and involving the destruction of the offenders' houses. These can be caused by those who tease or laugh at animals. *Vide Studies in Religion, Folk-lore and Custom*, pp. 153–154, 199–207.

beautiful clothes. There is also a dragon under the earth. When *talain* is feared, blood is drawn from the skin with a working-knife, and the blade then thrust into the ground. Some blood is also thrown aloft. Agila wood is burnt, and the smoke taken in the hands and blown towards the sky.

The Chimloi-i[1] come from Bonsu. They look like Negritos, but can become birds or centipedes. They go to the shaman (*halak*).

The spirit of a dead person leaves the body by the head, or breast or back. The ghost is like "one of us." It journeys to where the sun sets and then goes up.

The above account was obtained at Jeransang: the following information is from Lom, a young Negrito of Lata Lang:

When a man dies, his spirit goes up to the sky in the west. When the spirit is going up, the relatives and friends hold a magical singing performance. Jawait meets the spirit, and tells it to play at tops and wrestle (Malay *bĕrsilat*). He invites it to eat fruit. The spirit gets the juice of the *pĕrah*-tree and tattoos its face with this[2]. It takes flowers and puts them on its head. Afterwards it becomes a bird, a *chekeb* (? Argus pheasant), a *tekem* (a species of hornbill), a chow-hut (?) or a *chip-chib* (?).

The *Badan pakon*[3] (a bird which the Perak Malays call *kangkang katup*, from its note) is also the soul of a dead man. It calls the durian flowers to appear.

Jawait has a wife, Geles, who lives with him in the sky.

Below the earth is a dragon which makes *talain*. If we laugh at, or play with, ants, *talain* comes.

My elderly informant at Jeransang would not admit the accuracy of some of Lom's statements. He said that only

---

[1] For beliefs of the Perak Negritos about these beings (*chinoi*), *vide Studies in Religion*, etc., pp. 148, 150–151, 160–167, 171–174, 186; also *infra*, pp. 24, 25, 27, 28.

[2] The Cheka Negritos both tattoo and paint their faces. Tattooing is usually done with soot of some kind, the face-painting with the gummy juice of some tree, which often removes the skin underneath, resulting in a temporary scar. I suspect that face-painting may be meant in this case, though the Malay word *cholek* ("to prick") was used to describe the operation.

[3] A cuckoo; probably *Cuculus concratus*.

the ghosts of shamans could meet Jawait, and that he did not know of Geles.

A Negrito Burial

It may sound hard-hearted to say so, but it was lucky for me that a Jeransang Negrito had died a few days before I arrived. I was thus enabled to visit the grave, and to learn much more than I could have done from mere descriptions. The encampment in which the people were living at the time of my visit was not more than a couple of hundred yards from the place where the man had died. He had been buried in his own shelter, and the others had deserted the camp. This, by the addition of palm leaves, had been turned into a beehive-like structure, so that it was impossible to get a glimpse of the inside. I was told that the corpse had been buried, but the grave must have been shallow, as a distinct and unpleasant odour could be detected, though not very strongly.

My old instructor in Negrito lore refused to go near the grave, unless he got a dollar for doing so, as he was frightened. I paid him a dollar, but "took it out of him" rather unmercifully afterwards, by teasing him, in front of some Malays, with having suffered from a dollar's worth of fright.

A well-marked path led from the grave to the new encampment, and certain objects set beside this track conclusively proved that the Negritos are frightened of the dead man's spirit. Apart from this, I was told that in the singing performance at the end of seven days, when the soul is supposed to be passing to the other world, it is instructed not to loiter near the houses of the survivors. The objects intended to prevent the spirit visiting the camp of his relations were a sapling felled across the path and four "tigers" made of palm leaves. The "tigers" were placed in pairs. They were single leaves, the petioles of which had been planted in the ground so that the under sides were directed towards the grave. The leaflets had then been drawn downwards and plaited, or knotted, together. Close to the pair of "tigers" furthest from the grave was a model wind-break, under the shelter of which was a little cooked rice in a coconut-shell, this being food for the ghost.

I was told that a working-knife, an adze, mats and "clothes" are placed in the grave with the corpse, but the blade of the knife should have a broken tang, and the mat and adze should be worn out; for the ghost considers a broken knife good, a new one useless. This is, of course, an instance of "dead" articles for the use of a dead man.

The corpse is said to be buried with its face towards the setting sun. As far as I could ascertain, the usual custom, when a man dies, is for the Negritos to move camp to a little distance immediately, and then again—further off—after the singing performance, which assists his migration to a better world.

Playing on musical instruments is forbidden during the period between a death and the soul's departure from the earth. A Malay who accompanied me suggested to the Negritos that he would like to hear them play one of their stringed instruments, but he was told that they could not do so, as they were still in the tabued period.

The Shaman

"The shaman (*halak*) performs in the dark and holds a sprout of the *salak*-palm in his hands. Long, but very fine, cords are attached to his finger-nails, toe-nails and breast. These stretch to heaven, to Bonsu. When the magical performance is over, the threads go back to Bonsu, who let them down to the *halak* in the first place." This account is from an old Negrito of Jeransang and varies somewhat from that of Lom, of Lata Lang, which is given below:

"The *halak* sits on a mat. He holds *salak* palm (*bekod*) leaves in his hands to take hold of a fine cord (? cords) which come down from heaven. The cord is sharp and would cut his hand if he did not use the leaves. Jawait[1] lets down the cord when he hears people holding a séance. He lives in the 'eye of heaven' and tells the *halak* to climb the cord to him.

[1] Bonsu according to my other informant.

He has a big beard which sometimes appears white, sometimes green. He is, too, sometimes young, sometimes old."

Magical Patterns on Girdles

While at Jeransang, I purchased two women's girdles of rattan, these being decorated with rudely scratched-in patterns. These patterns, I was told, protect the wearer against pains in the small of the back. Rough sketches of some of them, together with their names, are given below. Some bamboo combs (*kenaid*) were also bought. The patterns on these are very roughly executed, and in no way like those to be found on Negrito combs from Perak. I was informed that the comb patterns had no magical use.

Jekob jengloi (a snake which the Malays call *ongkok sampah*)

Luie (bees)

Jĕkob yasun (snake with red tail and head)

Jĕkob penungai (a kind of snake)

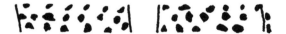

Ka klai (the fish which the Malays call *bujok*)

PLATE II

Author's photograph

NEGRITO WOMEN IN WIND-BREAK
Jeransang, Pahang

Author's photograph

NEGRITO WOMEN OF JERANSANG
Note face-paint and rattan belt with magical patterns on
woman on left. The left-hand woman in the top picture
also has her face painted

PLATE III

Author's photograph

"TIGERS" AND SOUL HUT AT JERANSANG

The "tigers" are the two plaited leaves (A and B).
The little domed soul hut (C) can just be

Author's photograph

NEGRITO GRAVE AT JERANSANG

The actual grave is under the wind-break, which
has been covered in with palm leaves

III. SOME BELIEFS OF THE NEGRITOS OF LENGGONG, PERAK

The following notes are the result of a short visit to the Negritos of Lenggong. Their meagreness is partly accounted for by the fact that I could not find, as I did previously at Selama, an informant who was able to give me very connected evidence, to the temporary desertion of the camp near Lenggong by its inhabitants, who went to clear jungle-reserve boundaries in the neighbourhood of Kuala Kenering, and to an attack of fever from which the only male left behind suffered. This man, Pandak, is a son of Dahabok, a Negrito with whom von Grübauer had dealings in connection with obtaining skeletal material (*Pagan Races*, vol. I, p. 581). Dahabok is reported to have contracted leprosy. He died some years ago, and I knew him fairly well before he suffered from the disease.

Pandak, though willing to help me, was not a good man to work with, as he had the greatest difficulty in telling a straightforward story. What material I got from him is supplemented, to a certain extent, by matter obtained from men of the same camp who came with him to see me at one time or another, and by that from an elderly man whom I had previously met at Ijok in Selama, but who, at the time of my visit to Lenggong, was living with To' Singha's people in the Gua Badak[1] ("Rhinoceros's Cave") near Sumpitan.

In reading this paper comparison should be made with former information obtained at Ulu Selama which has appeared in my *Studies in Religion, Folk-lore and Custom*.

The Negrito Gods

Tapern has a white skin. He lives in a cave in the sky. Tabung (the dragonfly) tells him when human beings are committing offences and he then throws down a huge quartz

---

[1] About four miles from Lenggong.

crystal which goes into the earth, and the waters well up from the hole which it makes and drown the offenders.

Yara-meng is a female being who lives in the sky. She is white and very aged, just "skin and bone." Her grand-daughter, Jamoi, looks after her, and when she has reached the extreme limits of old age Jamoi makes as if to strike her from afar with some wild ginger (*beurn*[1]) leaves. The sap, coming from the stalks of the leaves, falls upon Yara-meng, who feels cold when thus besprinkled, and immediately becomes young again.

The Sun

The sun goes under the earth when it sets. Yak (grand-mother) Pudau guards the place where it rises.

The Kĕpayang-tree and the Bridge

A curious story was told to me by Pandak, of which I could not get a full explanation. He said that near the place where the sun rises there is a *kĕpayang* (*hod*) tree[2]. From close to the base of the tree there stretches a bridge (*galong*[3]) which extends towards a fire—"the original fire"—called *Jamput*. For some reason, the tree went (or goes) to the other side of the fire, avoiding the bridge, and going round. The tree becomes a *Chinoi* at night. Yara-meng came out of its roots, and it was, at first, a snake.

Thunder (Punishment Tales)

I have already referred to the welling up of water caused by Tapern throwing down a quartz crystal. Such acts as laughing at a cat or dog are extremely displeasing to the Powers Above and, as a punishment, bad thunderstorms with floods of rain are sent, which when thus produced are

---

[1] *Tĕpus* was the Malay word used for "wild ginger," but there are several species of which *beurn* (a Negrito name) is one.

[2] *Kĕpayang* is the Malay name of the tree, *hod* the Negrito name. According to Ridley the *kĕpayang* is *Pangium edule*.

[3] Perhaps the "bridge of the rising sun" referred to in a Kintak Bong song. *Vide Studies in Religion*, etc., p. 162.

called *h'moin*[1]. These are followed by phenomena called *henwoie*[2] which comprise the welling up of water and the engulfing of the offenders' camp in the earth. Tajuk ("snake") looks after the waters under the earth, and Pandak said with regard to this snake, "If we don't pay him, he kills us," this being with reference to the blood-throwing ceremony for averting *henwoie*. According to Pandak, it is Yara-meng who takes the blood which is thrown upwards[3].

An enormous green grasshopper, of the kind which the Malays call *bĕlalang kochong*, makes thunder with its wings.

Chinoi

There are many *Chinoi* of different kinds and of the same kind. *Chinoi* look like children and are, Pandak said, "about two and a half feet high." There are Hornbill *Chinoi* and Vulture *Chinoi*. A *Chinoi* takes up its abode in the body of a bird, and, when it wishes, it comes out again. The kind of banana which the Malays call *pisang toman* has *Chinoi*, so too has the tapioca plant. *Chinoi* originate in a small species of wild ginger, called *beurn* (*vide* footnote *supra*, p. 24). A cavity forms in the stem of the plant, and this is filled with water. The water gives rise to a small stone[4], the stem of the plant swells and cracks, and the stone becomes a *Chinoi*.

The *Chinoi* are used by the *bĕlian* (shaman who can become a wer-tiger) in his séances, and, according to Pandak, they enter his body.

The Abode of the Dead and their Journey to it

One informant (Pandak) told me that the spirits of the dying leave the bodies either by the big toe or by the top of the head, but another said they come out of the whole body and have the appearance of human beings, but are white.

---

[1] Equivalent to the Malay word *chĕlau*.
[2] Equivalent to *kĕlĕboran* (Malay) which follows upon *chĕlau*.
[3] For particulars of the blood-throwing ceremony among the Negritos *vide Studies in Religion*, etc., pp. 151–152.
[4] A quartz crystal. I have recently purchased a specimen from a Negrito of Lenggong which he used in curing illness by administering to the patient water in which it had been steeped.

The ghosts, according to the same man, go to paradise by themselves, though sometimes the spirits of their fathers come and take them away. Pandak told me that paradise (*laud*), of which Yak (grandmother) Chin is in charge, is situated near the place where the sun falls, and that there are many flowers there. The *Mapik*-tree, which grows in paradise, has red *tanjong* flowers on one side of it and *Hibiscus* flowers on the other. The spirits of the dead go to *laud* on the seventh night after death, but, before they go, feed themselves by rubbing banana ashes on their throats. They do not feed by the mouth like human beings.

When a death occurs in a camp, it is immediately deserted, but the people may return to the same neighbourhood after the elapse of two months. The body of a *bĕlian* (wer-tiger) must not be buried. It must be placed on a platform in the hut in which death took place. The corpses of ordinary persons, according to my Gua Badak informant, are buried lying on their backs, with their heads pointing to where the sun goes down.

The Bird-Soul

The call of a species of woodpecker, *hilai*, denotes that friends are coming; that of the *bakau* (the same, I believe, as the *til-tol-tapah* of the Ulu Selama Negritos) that a child will be born.

One species of hawk is thought to have an evil spirit which is especially dangerous to young children. Pandak told me that his people moved to their then location (on a hill above Lenggong) from their former camp, because of the constant presence of hawks, which caused the children to be sickly. The hawk's shadow seems to be particularly feared.

FOLK-TALES

Tak Kiem, Yak Gadong and Jati

There was once an old couple, whose names were Tak (grandfather) Kiem and Yak (grandmother) Gadong. They had eyelashes but no eyeballs. They were having connection under the impression that it was still night, though it was really daylight, because their grandson, Jati, had told them that it was dark. When it was about midday the grandson told his grandparents that it was day. Then the grandson caught his grandmother by the leg and carried her down into the water, and, when she became cold, her eyes could see, and she wept. Then she sprang to a mountain top and became a *Chinoi*. The grandfather became a tiger. The grandson told his grandfather not to speak like an ox, a barking-deer, or any other animal, but like a tiger, "Aung." The tiger-grandfather looks after this country—Lenggong—which we call *Kemoin*, and makes springs of water by shooting arrows into the rocks.

Yak Taneg

Yak (grandmother) Taneg was ill and died. Before she died she told her children to go and dig tubers in the hollow[1]. Her five children went to the place where the tubers were, a daughter taking a young child with her. When they got there, they met Yak Taneg's ghost in the hollow. The children said, "We five children have come here"; and Yak Taneg told them to make a fire and roast the tubers without cleaning them. So they roasted them. Now the youngest of Yak Taneg's five children was a *bĕlian*, and he told the others not to go far from the fire, but to sit close together, because Yak Taneg wanted to take away their tongues and kill them. Yak Taneg was still sitting in the hollow and, when she was given the tubers, which had not been cleaned, she took the charcoal from them and smeared it all over her body. Then she came out of the hollow and chased her children, but the son who was a *bĕlian* hit her with a *palas*-shoot, and she went away. Then the children wept because the *bĕlian* said that their mother was dead. So they went home, and the *bĕlian* told them to make a "medicine-hut," and that night he went into it and, after he had called his *Chinoi* to him, he invoked his mother to come down into the hut to see the decorations

---

[1] The Malay word used for hollow was *jĕlok*.

which were in it, doing this because he wished her to become a *Chinoi*, and not to remain a ghost. When his mother came down from above and plunged into the hut, the *Chinoi* of the *bĕlian* caught hold of her and one of them blew sap of the *sĕlaseh*-plant[1] over her; whereupon she became a *Chinoi*, and the *bĕlian* took her to the sky.

[1] A fragrant herb, *Ocimum basilicum*. The Malay name is *sĕlaseh*.

IV. ON AN EXAMINATION OF SOME NEGRITO COMBS FROM PERAK

The commonest types of comb that I have collected from the Kintak Bong of the Ulu Selama parish of Perak are the six- and the eight-pattern varieties. In both of these the kinds of patterns, their arrangement with regard to one another, and their comparative sizes, are all regulated by tradition.

Let us take first of all a six-pattern comb, such as is shown on Plate IV, fig. A. The pattern of the first panel stands by itself, not being reproduced elsewhere on the comb. Pattern 2, however, recurs again in panel 6, and pattern 3 in panel 5. The fourth pattern—different from any of the others—is always much larger than the rest. Now it is in accordance with tradition that only a few kinds of patterns are allowable in panel 1, and the same is true for the similar panels 2 and 6, 3 and 5, as well as for panel 4.

In the ordinary type of eight-pattern (or eight-panel) comb the arrangement is similar, except that two extra panels, containing the same patterns as panels 2 and 6 of the six-pattern comb (2 and 8 in the eight-pattern comb) are inserted, one on either side of the largest panel—panel 4 in a six-pattern comb. We may, therefore, since it is understood that an eight-pattern comb is exactly the same as a six-pattern, except for the addition of the two extra panels, as remarked, leave this type and proceed to the detailed examination of the patterns which are to be found on six-panel combs.

The whole comb is called *kenait*, the panels *papan*[1], and the boundary lines between the patterns *enem*. In panel 4, according to my Kintak Bong informant, the following patterns are allowable: "crossing jackfruit shoots" (*tenwug nangka*), "cucumber flowers," "thighs of the monitor-lizard" (*bleuk patiu*), "young moon" (*wong*[2] *kichek*), "breast

---

[1] A Malay word which means "plank."   [2] *Wong* means "child."

of the red-breasted hill tortoise" (*sob sueh*) and "bracken leaves" (*hilik yawin*). Probably the commonest of these is *tenwug nangka.*

In panels 2 and 6 the commonest pattern is *kebeurk padi* (padi grains) though *tapag salag* (leaflets of the Salak[1]) is sometimes found, as also "gourd seeds," a pattern very similar to "padi grains" but in which the diamonds, which are often shorter and broader, have a dot in the centre of each. Leaf-monkey's teeth (*yus ai*) is the almost invariable pattern in panels 3 and 5, while panel 1 may have *pisuas chinbeg* (torn-open cabbage of the Bertam-palm[2]), *gel talung* (millipedes' waists), *sudak taduk* (spikes of the Bayas-palm[3]) or *sudak manau* (spikes of the Rotan manau[4]). A study of combs collected in the Ulu Selama parish, and now in the Perak Museum—ten specimens—gives the following results:

Nos. 1, 2, 3. Typical eight-panel combs.

Nos. 4, 5, 6, 7. Typical six-panel combs.

No. 8. Typical six-panel comb, except that panel 2 has the pattern which is called "cucumber seeds," while panel 6 has the ordinary "padi grains." These two divisions, therefore, do not "balance" one another.

No. 9. Typical six-panel comb with cucumber seeds in panels 2 and 6.

No. 10. An eight-panel comb. Non-typical. Evidently the production of a prentice hand. Three panels blank, and patterns, which are merely rudely engraved, not of the usual type.

A very noticeable feature of Perak Negrito decorative art as applied to bamboo is that, whereas the Sakai usually merely scratches the skin of the bamboo to make patterns, afterwards colouring the scratches slightly with some brownish or blackish substance, the Negrito, to obtain more outstanding effects, often removes parts of the light yellow skin of the plant and colours the underlying portions a rich brown. Some patterns produced in this way are to be found on nearly every bamboo article made by the Perak Negritos, and though

---

[1] The *Salak*-palm, *Zalacca edulis*. *Salak* is the Malay name.

[2] *Eugeissona tristis*.   [3] *Oncosperma horrida*.

[4] The Malay name of a kind of rattan palm.

many designs are merely made by scratching the skin, those in which the skin has been removed give Negrito bamboo articles a very distinctive appearance. When this process is employed the yellow skin may either form a pattern which stands out against a dark brown background, or may provide a light background which shows up a dark pattern. A good example of the former type of ornamentation is the pattern called "padi grains": in this the yellow diamond-shaped grains are in strong contrast with the brown background. In the "monkey teeth" pattern, on the other hand, the brown pattern (teeth) contrasts with a yellow background.

An examination of Negrito combs from other parts of North Perak—the places from which we have examples are Ijok (Selama Sub-District) and Lenggong and Grik in Upper Perak—would seem to show that the rules stated above are more or less observed in these places also, for, though there are examples which do not conform to type, it is to be noticed that these are very often the worst in execution and design, and, probably, are the work of juveniles, or of inexpert adults. According to the evidence of Tōkeh[1], a Menik Kaien Negrito living at Ijok, the traditional Negrito comb patterns were obtained from Yak Tanggoi[2], a deified Kintak Bong ancestress, who now resides in the sky with Tapern. She it was who first taught the Negritos to make combs and other personal ornaments, and mothers still say to their girl children, when they are inclined to consider themselves good-looking, and be conceited in consequence, "You need not think that you are as beautiful as Yak Tanggoi."

I have found absolutely no evidence that engraved combs are regarded as talismans by the Negritos of Perak, though the patterns on the dart-quivers are thought to make the game tame, so that it may easily be shot by the hunters with their blowpipes. Tōkeh told me, in 1921, that the Negritos decorated their quivers with such patterns as they dreamt would prevent game becoming frightened.

---

[1] Obtained in 1921.
[2] Yak Tanggoi means "Grandmother Rambutan."

Patterns in the Illustrations

(a) Torn-open cabbage of the Bertam palm (*pisuas chinbeg*).
(b) Padi grains (*kebeurk padi*).
(c) Teeth of the lotong monkey (*yus ai*).
(d) Crossing *shoots of the* jackfruit (*tenwug nangka*).
(e) Leaflets of the Salak palm (*tapag salag*).
(f) Thighs of the monitor-lizard (*bleuk patiu*).
(g) Millipedes' waists (*gel talung*).
(h) Cucumber flowers ⎫
(i) Bertam pattern   ⎬ Names obtained in Malay only.
(j) Gourd seeds   ⎪
(k) Birds' wings   ⎭

With regard to these patterns, it will be noted that there is a great similarity between *pisuas chinbeg* (a) and the design which I have called "Bertam pattern." *Pisuas chinbeg*, according to my informant, means "torn-open *cabbage of the* Bertam-palm," while the Malay name obtained for it was *bunga bertam*[1], *bunga* meaning either "flower" or "pattern[2]."

With reference to (g), the name given—"millipedes' waists" (*gel talung*)—is rather doubtful.

The patterns (f) (*bleuk patiu*) in comb C and those (d) termed *tenwug nangka* in combs A and B, are almost identical, though in comb A there are four dots placed in the centre of the diamond formed by the crossing elements of the pattern. I believe that the elongated diamonds of comb A are less typical of *tenwug nangka* than the form found in comb B.

It may be remarked here that the F.M.S. Museums possess no examples of Negrito combs from the Eastern States of the Peninsula, except some, in Taiping, from the Batek of Jeransang and of the Cheka River, Pahang. These specimens are, however, not at all typical of Negrito art.

---

[1] From a Negrito of Grik, from whom the comb was bought.
[2] Compare these two patterns with that which I have queried (Plate IV).

PLATE IV

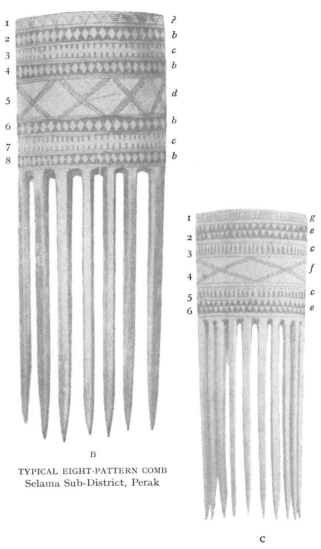

A

TYPICAL SIX-PATTERN COMB
Selama Sub-District, Perak

B

TYPICAL EIGHT-PATTERN COMB
Selama Sub-District, Perak

C

TYPICAL SIX-PATTERN COMB
Selama Sub-District, Perak

PLATE V

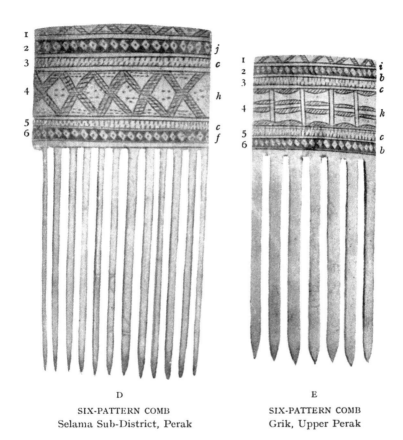

D

SIX-PATTERN COMB
Selama Sub-District, Perak

E

SIX-PATTERN COMB
Grik, Upper Perak

V. VAUGHAN STEVENS AND THE PATTERNS ON NEGRITO COMBS

In the course of work among the Negritos, I have frequently had necessity to refer to Vaughan Stevens's material as quoted, and sometimes interpreted, by Skeat. A number of mistakes in this appear to be due to genuine misunderstanding of the Negritos by Vaughan Stevens; while Skeat, when attempting to throw light on obscure matters, appears occasionally to have complicated affairs by incorrect comments which owe their origin to his not having worked in the neighbourhood where the information was obtained. In the following notes I essay some elucidations, and also suggest comparisons with material to be found in my *Studies in Religion, Folk-lore and Custom in British North Borneo and the Malay Peninsula* as well as in the preceding paper.

First of all, with regard to the patterns on bamboo combs, I must state that as yet I have obtained absolutely no confirmation of Vaughan Stevens's "flower theory" (*Pagan Races of the Malay Peninsula*, W. W. Skeat and C. O. Blagden, vol. I, pp. 396–401). Skeat, however, says (*t.c.* p. 429) that "the drawings and combs collected by Vaughan Stevens are nearly all from the East Semang or Pangan, and are all very typical specimens of the work of the east-coast Negritos, though they are not all made by the men; a single specimen was obtained from the Semang of Perak and two others were also collected on the west side of the Peninsula." Vaughan Stevens also says that the magical meaning of the comb patterns has been forgotten by the Negritos of the west coast (*t.c.* p. 420).

Unfortunately, my knowledge of the Malay States Negritos, except with regard to two groups in Pahang which do not make typical combs, is limited to those of the west coast and, furthermore, the F.M.S. Museums do not, with the exception of some objects from the above-mentioned Pahang group, contain any examples of the arts and crafts of the Negritos on the eastern side of the main range. On the appearance of many of the combs illustrated by Vaughan Stevens, however, I should certainly consider them to have been collected in the west of the Peninsula, and the pattern names are in numerous cases identical with, or very similar to, those which I have obtained in the Ulu Selama, Perak, or from Negritos of Upper Perak. Of those figured by Skeat (after Vaughan Stevens) I should describe Nos. 15 B, 17 A, 17 B, 18 D, 19 A, 19 B, 19 C, 19 E, 19 G, 19 H, 19 J, 19 K, 19 L, 19 M and 19 N of the plate which faces p. 427 in vol. I of *Pagan Races,* as typical examples of the work of the Negritos of Perak, but I have, as stated, no east-coast material for comparative purposes. It is, however, known that Vaughan Stevens worked in the Ulu Selama[1] whence these combs might very well have come.

Vaughan Stevens says that the fifth panel of a Negrito comb contains a pattern which is intended to represent a disease against which it protects its wearer (*t.c.* pp. 426, 427). This is the fifth and largest panel in an eight-panel comb, for in a six-panel comb the largest panel becomes number four. Certain of these "diseases," taken from Vaughan Stevens's work, are illustrated by Skeat, and notes on them are appended (*t.c.* pp. 606–617). In the following paragraphs Vaughan Stevens's notes, as translated by Skeat, are in italics:

Pagan Races, vol. I, p. 608:

5 A. *Disease, "pasar chin-beg" ("Passar chin-beg"), unexplained, cp. "Li-chin-beg" ("Lee-chin-beg"): "disease of the upper jaw."*
I suggest "pisuas chinbeg," torn-open cabbages of the Bertam-palm (*vide supra,* p. 32). Not a disease at all.

T.c. p. 609:

12 A. *Disease, "Chas-ai" ("Chaseye"), unidentified.* This is really "chas ai," hands of the lotong-monkey. For confirmatory evidence (*vide* vocabularies in vol. II of *Pagan Races,* p. 626), no. 14 (*chas*) and p. 659, no. 140 (*ai*).

---

[1] *Vide Papers on Malay Subjects, The Aboriginal Tribes,* by R. J. Wilkinson, p. 4.

T.c. p. 610:

17 A. *Disease, "Tin-weg Langka" ("Tinwag-langkar"), unidentified.* This is, almost certainly, "tenwug nangka," crossing shoots of the jack-fruit tree. "Nangka" is ordinary Malay for the jack-fruit tree, and "tenwug" is Negrito for a cross-pattern. (*Vide supra,* p. 32 and Plate IV; also *Studies in Religion, Folk-lore and Custom,* p. 159, with reference to the meaning of "tenwug.")

T.c. p. 610:

19 A. *Disease, "Bakau timun" ("Bakow Timoon"), unidentified.* "Timun (cucumber) flowers." (*Vide supra,* p. 32 and Plate V.) "Bakau" is the ordinary Negrito word for flower: "timun" is Malay for cucumber. Vaughan Stevens's pattern agrees with mine.

T.c. p. 614:

50. *Disease, "Ka-hib," unidentified.* "Centipede." (*Vide Pagan Races,* vol. II, p. 555, no. 66.)

T.c. p. 614:

57. *Disease, "Geltalung" or "Jeltalung" ("Gel-taloong"), unidentified.*
The translation given to me (in Malay) for this pattern name was "millipedes' waists." (*Vide supra,* p. 32) and *Pagan Races,* vol. II, p. 750, "Waist (Mal. pinggang): gel (*pr* gell), *Pang. U. Aring."*

I have thus shown that where I am able to give translations of these pattern names, they are not those of diseases as stated by Vaughan Stevens: nor have I, up to the present, any information to the effect that they are of any use in warding off sickness.

Among other pattern names collected by Vaughan Stevens, and recorded in *Pagan Races,* my translations of several are given below together with confirmatory references to the comparative vocabularies in vol. II of *Pagan Races:*

Pagan Races, vol. I, pp. 615, 616:

Boin ⎫
Boing ⎭ monkey, *P.R.* vol. II, p. 659, no. 134.
Sob, breast, *P.R.* vol. II, p. 544, no. 380.
Awin ("*Ow-in*"), bamboo, *P.R.* vol. II, pp. 522, no. 29.

T.c. p. 616:

Kelau-wong or "Keluwang" ? ("*Klow-wang*"), 65 [? = *bat*]. A kind of fruit, unidentified, known to the Patani Malays as "*kenuwak*" (*Studies in Religion, Folk-lore and Custom,* p. 172).

One or two points in connection with the provenance of a few of the combs can be elucidated. On p. 612, 25 A, of *Pagan Races* Skeat quotes certain notes of Vaughan Stevens which are supplemented, in one case, by some remarks either by Skeat or by Vaughan Stevens's German editors, probably by the former. The following is the single example:

Tribe: Semang of Kinta ("Kintar," Ulu Kinta being a Sakai locality).

There can, I think, be no doubt at all that a mistake in interpretation has been made. Ulu Kinta *is* a Sakai locality, but Vaughan Stevens evidently collected his specimen from the Kintak Negritos. Kintak is a tribal designation. The Ulu Selama group calls itself "Kintak Bong," while the Negritos of Kroh in Upper Perak, when I asked them what name they applied to themselves, replied "Kintak." They are, however, doubtfully the true Kintak (said to frequent the neighbourhood of the Kupang River in Kedah) but, as in the case of the Kintak Bong, some qualifying epithet is probably added. In this case the patterns were most likely collected at Belum, as 25 B, the next example, is definitely stated to have come from that locality.

With regard to the specimen 25 C, on the same page, a note, as follows, is appended:

Tribe: Semang of Bong.

This pattern is evidently from the Kintak Bong of Ulu Selama and the neighbourhood:

25 D *Tribe: Semang of Ken-Siu ("Ken-Siew") and East Semang ("Orang Panggang").*

The Kinsieu are stated to live in the neighbourhood of Baling and Siong in Kedah. (*Vide Studies in Religion, Folklore and Custom*, p. 145.)

VI. THE KĔRAU RIVER SAKAI-JAKUN, RELIGION AND CUSTOM

This slight account of the beliefs and customs of the Sakai-Jakun of the Kĕrau River, Pahang, was gathered partly from members of the group who, in 1921, were living on the Tembeling River near Jeram Ampai, partly from the inhabitants of a village called Galong, which is situated on the Kĕrau near Kuala Terbul—I visited these people when descending from Gunong (Mt.) Benom in 1923—and partly from certain men whom I met on the Kĕrau during a short visit in 1925.

The Kĕrau Sakai-Jakun are a non-Malay speaking division, but their physical characteristics seem to tend towards the Jakun type. Their legends, too, point to a southern origin, though there has probably been a good deal of admixture of Sakai and Negrito blood. These are known to the Negritos of the Jeransang and Cheka neighbourhoods as Jah, and claim originally to have come from Sumatra.

The following two accounts of their migrations were given to me in 1925:

(1) The Kĕrau people came from Pagar Ruyong in Sumatra. On entering the Peninsula they were led by two brothers and a sister. One brother settled in Johore, the other in Pekan, while their sister became Batin (chief—a Jakun title) of those of the people who settled on the Kĕrau.

(2) The Kĕrau people originally ran away from Pagar Ruyong because they were oppressed by the Malay raja, who continually ordered them to go into the jungle to search for ebony. They were so badly treated in the matter of this forced labour that they had not even time to plant rice; so they took ship and escaped to Pahang, settling in the Semantan neighbourhood. The raja sent his Temenggong and a noted warrior in chase of them to Pahang, but the fugitives refused to return.

They moved to the Kĕrau from the Semantan when there

was a quarrel among brothers—Malays (? Sultan Ahmad and his brother)—as to who should be ruler of Pahang. This was at the time of the "Rawa War."

They circumcise because this was a sign of submission to the raja when they lived at Pagar Ruyong.

There was, it is said, only one Batin on the Kĕrau: now there are two.

Plates and spears are the media in which tribal fines are paid. My Tembeling informant told me that the fine for murder was, or rather used to be, sixty-six spears, while incest in the worst degree, is said to have been punishable by a fine of one hundred and sixty spears. Other minor fines were—for stealing crops, one spear and one plate; unfaithfulness on a woman's part, six spears and two plates. Probably, judging by the abatements given below, payment in full of the largest fines was never enforced.

Spears and plates also form a part of the bride-price. Thus the nominal payment by a suitor to a father for the hand of a virgin daughter is sixty spears, but actually only from three to six are paid, the number varying according to the quality of the weapons. The bride-price for a widow is less, the nominal number of spears being fifteen, with two china plates. Only one spear and two plates are paid.

When a man divorces a woman he gives her one spear and one plate, while, if the woman asks for a divorce, she must pay back her bride-price.

Plates and spears appear to have a sort of currency value.

Males are said to be buried with their heads pointing down stream; females with heads up stream.

According to one account, fire is placed at the foot of a grave, morning and evening, for the first seven days after a burial. Another man told me—and there is very possibly some variation in custom—that for three days after death, seven little fires, contained in coconut shells, are kindled at the grave each night, and another seven, in similar receptacles, are placed on the dead man's mat within the house.

If a cat walks over a body which is awaiting burial it is thought that the dead person will arise, kill the inhabitants of the house, and will then return to the burial mat and again become a corpse. It is also said that the dead, if not watched before burial, will arise and tear the living to pieces.

A dead person, before burial, and for three nights after, is a *kemoit*; after this a *bes*. A *bes* has the appearance of a living person. Thunder (*kareh*) is said to be the anger of *bes*.

The rainbow is a path for disease. If people are on a journey when a rainbow appears, they stop and build a small hut.

All males are circumcised at, or before, the age of puberty, but the operation, though apparently performed in the same manner as among Malays, is not so radical. I was told that the women do not undergo the corresponding rite.

Malay *mudin* (circumcisers) are often called in to operate. The Kĕrau people, however, in no way regard the operation as signifying admission to the faith of Islam.

The magician performs his rites in a round hut of palm leaves. Two are said to be usually built, one in the house of the sick man for whose benefit the performance is being held, one on the ground near the house. Such a séance had been held not long before my arrival at Galong and the remains of a "medicine-hut" were to be seen within the fence which surrounded one of the houses. I purchased the decorations, presumably offerings, which were hung from a model skeleton house, "the spirits' hall"—*balai hantu* in Malay. These include wooden models of elephants and tigers, the legs of which are attached to the bodies by means of pegs, and two model elephants made of fibrous cord wound round and round. Other ceremonial objects similarly obtained were a roughly made wooden spoon, a wooden model of a pair of pincers (such as Malays call *sĕpit*), a curiously but roughly carved piece of wood called a *Kabong*-palm trunk (*kreung kabong*), another rudely carved object said to be a fan, but not recognizable as such to the uninitiated, a small wooden dish and a rectangular piece of wood (a "lime tree trunk"), into which "branches" had been inserted in fours. On each branch was placed a very conventionalized wooden bird, a swallow (*chem samar*). A very similar, but somewhat larger "bird," of which only a single example was obtained, was called *chem laken*. From the base of the "lime tree trunk" sprang a downwardly curved piece of wood carved to represent a string of beetles. There were, probably, four of such decorations inserted in the base of the "lime tree," since the slots for them remain, but as these objects had been discarded after use, they were in many cases much damaged.

Other interesting specimens belonging to the series were plaited bands of palm leaves ("centipedes' fingers") and a long and elaborately plaited band of *Pandanus* which is stretched, probably from one of the house-posts, to the spirit-house and forms the road along which the spirit of the "medicine-man" comes.

Two switches of *palas*-leaves, which are used by him in calling his familiar, were also secured and a remarkable ceremonial headdress. This is illustrated on Plate VI and consists of "popped" rice threaded on fine cord.

PLATE VI

Author photograph

SAKAI-JAKUN, KĔRAU RIVER, PAHANG

Author's photograph

ABORIGINAL SHAMANS AND *BALAI HANTU*
Kĕrau River, Pahang

VII. THE JO-BEN OF THE LOMPAT RIVER, PAHANG

I first heard stories of a stone-implement-using wild people while on an expedition to the Tekam River, Pahang. My informant was a Malay named Woh, who was living with a group of pagans.

His statement about an unapproachable tribe, which is said to dwell around the head-waters of the Kĕrau, especially in the neighbourhood of the Lompat River, is of considerable interest. I obtained accounts of these people both from Woh and also from two Kĕrau River Sakai-Jakun, whom I met at Kuala Kĕrau while on the same expedition. The latter called them Cho-ben or Jo-ben, and said that they used fragments of stones, or sharpened stones, as implements. Woh, indeed, told me that he had once come upon one of their camps, which had been deserted on his approach, and found there pieces of stone with which they had been cutting thatch (*atap*). One of the Kĕrau men said that the Jo-ben used stones fixed in the ends of sticks[1] to dig with, and that their knives were made of bamboo. There is also a story that the Kĕrau Sakai-Jakun once caught a woman of the tribe, who was surprised while she was climbing a tree to obtain its fruit. She was said to have been tied up, but to have made her escape on the morning after her capture.

Now it is never wise to give too much credence to such tales; since it is well known what wonderful yarns the Malays and pagans—especially the former—spin about far-off tribes, which generally prove without truth when the tribes are visited; yet there are one or two points in them which are worth consideration.

I am gradually coming to the conclusion that some, at any rate, of the stone implements found in the Peninsula are not of very great age, and it seems that there is just a possibility that very remote pagan groups may still use them, or at any rate use chips of stone, for various purposes.

[1] I showed two stone implements to the Kĕrau men, asking them what they were, but they did not recognize them as being made by the Jo-ben. They said that they were thunderbolts—the usual Malay belief too.

The fact that legends of tribes still employing such implements have been previously recorded by de Morgan and Hale, tends to show that, even if it is not true that there are any tribes who are still practically in the stone age at the present day, yet there were at a date not so remote but that stories with regard to their existence are still current.

In 1923, while on a journey from Raub, *via* Gunong (Mt) Benom, to Kuala Kĕrau, I passed the mouth of the Lompat River. As it was impossible, in the depleted state of my commissariat and in the time at my disposal, to make what might well prove a protracted expedition in search of the Jo-ben, I had to content myself with questioning some of the pagans at Kuala Jelai, where I spent a night. The following information was obtained.

There are two divisions of aborigines on the Lompat, both wild. The first, the Maroi, are said to be similar in appearance to the Kĕrau pagans, but to speak a different dialect: they make houses and clearings. The second, the So-ben (Jo-ben and Cho-ben of my previous informants) are very wild, live in shelters and do not cultivate the soil. They are said to use stone knives, cutting and splitting wood with them. Stones of suitable shape are chosen from the bed of some river.

In 1925 I paid a further short visit to the mouth of the Lompat River, with a view, if possible, of finding out whether the Jo-ben really existed and of attempting, if time permitted, to get into touch with them. Unfortunately, the best information that I could obtain was not encouraging, and I was told by a Kĕrau pagan, named Hitam, who was supposed to know the Lompat well, that, though stories of these people were told, nobody had ever seen them. He offered, however, if I could wait for seven days, to bring in some members of another tribe, apparently Negritos. Having to return to Kuala Lumpur by the end of the month, which was then drawing to a close, I could not accept his offer.

I may remark here that Mr P. Phillips, late of the Forest Department, F.M.S., has also heard stories of the wild people on the Lompat who are credited with using stone implements.

VIII. A NOTE ON THE ORANG LAUT OF SINGAPORE

While in Singapore, in 1921, I paid a short visit to the village of Teluk Saga, which is situated off the shore of Pulau Brani, and opposite Tanjong Pagar Docks. The settlement consists of pile-dwellings standing in shallow water, and its inhabitants are said to be descendants of the Orang Laut, or Sea Gypsies, who were almost the only inhabitants of Singapore Island at the time of its occupation by Raffles.

My boatman, who himself belonged to the village, introduced me to the oldest inhabitant, one Amil bin Onil, an aged, but still fairly vigorous, man who told me that he was already selling corals to visitors to Singapore when there was "a one-legged Governor" there (Governor Cavanagh, 1861–67). As he was only a boy at the time, let us say from 12 to 14, he must now (in 1921) be in the neighbourhood of 70 years old. He said that his people were living in boats on the Singapore River, near the site of the present Government offices, when Raffles opened the new settlement, and that they migrated from there to Teluk Saga in Raffles' time. The head of the tribe, at that date, was named Wakin, and the grandfather of Amil was among those who moved to Pulau Brani. I understand that the people of the tribe originally acted as boatmen to the Běndahara.

Amil denied that there has been, or is, much mixture of local or foreign blood, Malay or other, among his people. They have, of course, long been converts to Islam.

The information derived from Amil is largely borne out by evidence to be found in *One Hundred Years of Singapore* (vol. I, pp. 342, 343).

IX. A NOTE ON THE SEA GYPSIES OF TRANG

During my visit to Peninsular Siam, in 1924, a very hurried visit was paid to some Sea Gypsies, living on an island named Pulau Peringai. These people, on casual inspection, seem to be typically Proto-Malays. They spoke Malay, and this appears to be their mother tongue, though it is likely that they use many words not to be found in Malay as ordinarily used in the Peninsula.

The Sea Gypsies are probably the group to whom the Trang-Patalung Negritos refer as Li. They build their houses raised from the ground and possess boats. The house roofings and wallings are of palm leaves. The settlement stood in a clearing which had contained dry-growing rice.

A few specimens only were purchased, these comprising a spear of palm wood—both blade and shaft being of this material and in one piece—several short, toy bamboo blowpipes, for shooting pellets; a bracelet made of the black seaweed which the Malays call *akar bahar*; an open *Pandanus* basket for rice, and a trident fish-spear. The last has a bamboo shaft and iron prongs, the centre prong being straight, the other two incurved and singly barbed on their inner surfaces. The above account is written from my specimens and from memory only: a few notes that I made have unfortunately been lost.

PART III

MALAY AND OTHER TECHNOLOGY

XII. NOTES ON THE MANUFACTURE OF DAMASCENED SPEAR AND KNIFE BLADES IN THE MALAY STATES

I HAD, some years ago, the good fortune to come across a Malay kĕris-smith's forge. The art of damascening as applied to the blades of weapons is rapidly dying out in all parts of the Peninsula, and is virtually extinct in so far as the Federated Malay States are concerned; therefore such facts as can still be gathered concerning an industry for which Malay craftsmen[1] of old were not unjustly celebrated should be put on record without delay. These notes consist entirely of personal observations, but those who wish to consult other papers should read the excellent account of kĕris-making by Dr R. O. Winstedt in the series of monographs on Malay subjects published by the Federated Malay States Government, and an article by Mr W. Rosenhain in vol. xxxi of the *Journal of the Anthropological Institute*, which deals largely with the microscopical aspect of the damascening as well as with the manufacture of blades. Both these communications are founded on notes taken by Mr W. W. Skeat in Trengganu. There is also a paper by Mr L. Wray in no. 3 of *Perak Museum Notes* "On the Malay Method of Colouring Kris and other Blades with Arsenic," which gives an account of the chemical combinations into which the arsenic enters with the different qualities of steel and iron of which Malay kĕris-blades are composed.

[1] Though Malay smiths of former days were undoubtedly skilled in kĕris-making, probably many of the very finest blades found in the Peninsula are of Javanese, Sumatran, or Bugis origin. It is doubtful if any considerable manufacture of weapons was ever carried on in any of the west coast states, though large numbers were turned out at Trengganu, and to a less extent in Kelantan and Patani.

it, and stretch it along the blade from the base of the *ganja*. Mark the point which it reaches with the left thumb-nail. Open the doubled strip and measure the breadth of the blade, exactly as above, marking out the strip of leaf into sections and repeating the same formula. Note what is the last word uttered.

Reverse the *kĕris*, so that its point is towards you, still holding it with the left hand. Take the other half of the original strip of leaf, double it and, placing one end of it on the *kĕris*-point, lay it along the blade. Mark the furthest point reached by placing your thumb-nail upon it, and measure the blade as before, the proximal edge of the leaf-strip being held under, or against, the thumb-nail. Note which is the last word uttered. The width of the blade has thus been measured at three points:

(*a*) at middle of blade;

(*b*) at a quarter-way from base;

(*c*) at a quarter-way from the tip.

For convenience we will call these the base, tip and middle measurements.

Now if the last word mentioned for all three measurements is *gunong*, this is unlucky, and the *kĕris* will be liable to catch in its sheath when its owner wishes to draw it upon an opponent; while if all three end on the word *runtoh* the *kĕris* will be liable to break when it is used in stabbing. If the three measurements, however, all end on the word *madu*, this is good and its owner's heart will be brave, though the weapon is not lucky to take on a trading expedition, nor to wear while doing agricultural work; while if all three end on *singgara*, that is the best of all, and everything that the wearer undertakes will be successful. Of the many other combinations of the four words which are obtainable the very worst is *gunong* for the measurement of the tip, while *singgara* and *runtoh* are also bad in this position, but not so bad as *gunong*. In these connections what words are obtained for the middle and base measurements are immaterial. To obtain *madu* for the point measurement is good, whatever the words for the middle and base may be.

All other combinations of the four words are fairly lucky.

(2) *Instructions for measuring a* kĕris *by another method.*

Information from Inche Wan Lela, Penghulu of Kuala Lipis, Pahang:

Take your *kĕris* and hold it by the blade, handle towards you. Place the right thumb crosswise at the base of the blade, then the left thumb above this. Next move the right thumb above the left, and again the left above the right, and so on, repeating the following verse, one section for each time either thumb is placed on the blade:

> *Ular berang | mĕniti riak.|*
> *Riak di-titi gĕlombang tujoh.|*
> *Karam di-laut, | timbul di-darat.|*
> *Habis utang, | bĕrganti utang.|*
> *Utang lama tiada bĕrbayar*[1].

Note to which part of the verse the last measurement of the *kĕris* falls. A piece of the *kĕris*-blade less than a thumb-breadth counts as a whole section.

If the last measurement falls to:

> *Ular berang* it is a good omen.
> *Mĕniti riak* it is a good omen.
> *Riak di-titi gĕlombang tujoh* it is a very good omen.
> *Karam di-laut* it is a very bad omen.
> *Timbul di-darat* it is a moderately good omen.
> *Habis utang* it is a good omen.
> *Bĕrganti utang* it is a bad omen.
> *Utang lama tiada bĕrbayar* it is a very bad omen.

[1] "The sea-snake bridges the ripples.
The ripples are bridged by the seven waves.
Wrecked at sea or floating ashore.
When you have finished your debts, you replace them with new ones, and old debts are left unpaid."

The *ular berang* is a fabulous sea-snake which is reported to be so deadly that, if it bites the rudder of a boat, or the oars, everybody in the boat will die, unless the part bitten is cut off.

(3) *Another Pahang method of measuring a* kĕris.

Information from Inche Wan Lela, Penghulu of Kuala Lipis. This method is very similar to no. 1, except that it is less complicated.

Measure length of blade from base to tip with a strip of *Pandanus* leaf. Cut strip to length measured. Fold strip double, and lay it along the blade from the base towards the point. Mark place reached by its distal end with left thumb-nail. Measure breadth of blade at this spot, keeping proximal edge of leaf-strip against, or just under, thumb-nail, and, as in the case of no. 1, divide up the leaf into sections, saying one of the following words or phrases for each section, and repeating until the end of the strip is reached:

Chĕnchala; mĕmbawa laba; pasupati; panah Rajuna; kĕtinggalan; kĕsĕsakan; anak raja kĕpanasan. Of these the omens are as follows:

Chĕnchala[1] (? meaning)	Good omen.
Mĕmbawa laba ("bringing rich returns")	Very good omen. The best possible.
Pasupati[2]	Good omen.
Panah Rajuna ("Arjuna's bow")	Good omen for use in war.
Kĕtinggalan ("left behind")	Very bad omen. The *kĕris* will always have been left behind when the owner encounters any trouble or danger.
Kĕsĕsakan ("indigence")	Very bad omen. The man who wears this weapon will never be in comfortable circumstances.
Anak raja kĕpanasan ("anger of royalty")	Omen not good for trading, but good in war. The wearer of this *kĕris* will not submit to rough speech and will be easily angered.

[1] Meaning unknown to Wan Lela.

[2] Dr P. van Stein Callenfels, of the Netherlands Indies Archaeological Service, informs me that Paçupati, originally a name of Çiva, meaning "Lord of Cattle," has become in Javanese and Malay literature the name of the magical arrow presented by Çiva to Arjuna. Note the reference to Arjuna's bow in the next phrase.

(4) *A fourth Pahang method of measuring a* kĕris.

Information from Inche Wan Lela, Penghulu of Kuala Lipis. Measure blade with a strip of *Pandanus* leaf from base to tip. Cut off this length, double it, and lay it along blade from base. Mark point reached with thumb-nail and measure breadth of blade here, as in other cases, repeating the process again and again until the end of the strip is reached. Then count into how many sections the *Pandanus* has been divided, and if there are either fourteen or sixteen sections the *kĕris* is unlucky.

(5) *A Perak method of measuring a* kĕris *to see if it will be lucky if taken on a trading expedition.*

From Pandak Ismail bin Anjang, a Malay of Batu Kurau, Perak:

Place the right thumb across base of *kĕris*-blade and the left directly above this. Move right thumb above left, then left above right, and so on, till the point of the blade is reached, repeating one of the following words, or phrases, for each time either thumb is placed on the blade:

> *Bĕrjun, bĕrkapal, bĕrsampan, putus tali;*
> *Bĕrubong, bĕrtampal, makan ta' mĕnchari.*

The omens and meanings of these words are as follows:

Bĕrjun[1] ("in a junk")	Good omen.
Bĕrkapal ("in a ship")	Good omen.
Bĕrsampan ("in a small boat")	Omen not very good.
Putus tali ("a broken cord")	Bad omen.
Bĕrubong ("joined up")	Omen not very good. Original capital will, perhaps, be lost, but fresh capital gained afterwards.
Bĕrtampal ("patched")	Omen not good. The owner of the *kĕris* will not be free of debts.
Makan ta' mĕnchari[2] (no necessity to search for food)	Omen good.

[1] It should be *bĕrjong*, but I give the word as it was pronounced by my informant, a Malay who knows nothing of the sea.

[2] *Makan ta' payah mĕnchari* would be more correct Malay, but this would break the run of the recitation.

Note that if there is a piece left over at the point of the *kĕris*, when measuring the blade, which is not sufficient to take the whole breadth of the thumb, this also counts as a full section, and a word, or phrase, must be said for it.

(6) *A Perak method for finding out whether any kind of* kĕris *or knife is good for use in war.*

Information from Pandak Ismail bin Anjang, a Malay of Batu Kurau, Perak:

Measure blade of weapon into sections with the thumbs, exactly as in the last instance, repeating, meanwhile, the following phrases, one for each measurement.

Anak buaya/mudik bĕrgĕntar./
Golok tĕrchĕpak¹/rimau tiba.

The omens and meanings of the phrases are as follows:

Anak buaya ("a young crocodile")	Omen good. The weapon will "fight well."
Mudik bĕrgĕntar (goes up stream shaking itself)	Omen bad. The weapon will not leave its sheath, though it will rattle in it as if loose.
Golok tĕrchĕpak (the knife is thrown away)	Omen bad.
Rimau tiba (and a tiger comes)	Omen bad.

(7) *To see if a* kĕris *will stab a tiger. A Perak method of measuring a weapon.*

Information from Pandak Ismail bin Anjang, a Malay of Batu Kurau, Perak.

Measure length of blade with a piece of cord, or a strip of leaf. Cut off cord to this length and double it. Place this doubled cord along blade from base upwards. Mark point reached by the distal end with left thumb-nail and measure breadth of blade repeatedly with the cord, as in the case of the Pahang instructions, but keep it doubled and measure from the ends, not from the loop. When the last measurement is reached, note whether the fold, where the cord is

¹ *Tĕrchĕpak* is equivalent to *tĕrchampak.*

doubled, coincides exactly with the edge of the *kĕris*. If it coincides, this is a good omen and the *kĕris*-blade will enter a tiger's body without difficulty. If it does not coincide, and there is a loop left over, try whether this loop is sufficiently large to admit the passage of the greater part of the blade. If it will admit it, the omen is good, and the *kĕris* may be used against a tiger, but, if it will not, and only the point of the *kĕris* will enter the loop, the blade will not pierce a tiger's body however hard a blow is given.

XI. TWO MALAY METHODS
OF DIVINATION

While staying at Lenggong, Upper Perak, in 1913, I attempted to see something of Malay magical practices, and, with this end in view, obtained the assistance of a Malay *kĕris*-smith, named Awang, who was doing some metal-work for me at the time. He got up several magical performances for my benefit, none of which was particularly impressive, but among them was an exhibition of divining by means of floating needles, which was given by an old woman.

The needles were thoroughly dried and then gently placed on the surface of water contained in a bowl. Care was taken not to break the surface-film of the water, so that the needles should not sink. They were then watched to see if they would come together or keep apart. From observations thus made, it is said that a girl who is betrothed can tell whether her marriage will result in a life-long partnership or will end in a divorce[1].

Divination by means of a ring is sometimes resorted to in an attempt to trace a thief. I have seen this method employed in Pahang. The chief performer was an elderly, blind man. The apparatus used consisted of a gold ring which was tied to a long hair—taken from a woman's head—and a basin. The basin was divided into eight compartments, internally, by four lines drawn with Indian ink, which crossed at its centre. In each compartment was written the name of a person who might possibly be the culprit. The unattached end of the hair was given to the blind man to hold with the thumb and index finger of his right hand and his hand was so placed that the ring hung suspended within the bowl, in the centre, and about half-way up. The old man then intoned an orthodox Mohammedan prayer, and, after this, the ring began to swing upon the hair.

When the test is successful the ring swings violently, and

[1] A similar method of divination is, or was, employed in India.

finally touches one of the sections containing a man's name. This man is considered to be the thief. On the occasion that I saw the performance, however, the ring, though it swung considerably, did not strike the side of the bowl, even when other names were twice substituted for the original eight. In consequence it was thought that the money which had been stolen had been taken by some one whose name was not included in those tried, though suspicion pointed very strongly to one of the men in the first eight.

PART III

MALAY AND OTHER TECHNOLOGY

XII. NOTES ON THE MANUFACTURE OF DAMASCENED SPEAR AND KNIFE BLADES IN THE MALAY STATES

I HAD, some years ago, the good fortune to come across a Malay kĕris-smith's forge. The art of damascening as applied to the blades of weapons is rapidly dying out in all parts of the Peninsula, and is virtually extinct in so far as the Federated Malay States are concerned; therefore such facts as can still be gathered concerning an industry for which Malay craftsmen[1] of old were not unjustly celebrated should be put on record without delay. These notes consist entirely of personal observations, but those who wish to consult other papers should read the excellent account of kĕris-making by Dr R. O. Winstedt in the series of monographs on Malay subjects published by the Federated Malay States Government, and an article by Mr W. Rosenhain in vol. XXXI of the *Journal of the Anthropological Institute*, which deals largely with the microscopical aspect of the damascening as well as with the manufacture of blades. Both these communications are founded on notes taken by Mr W. W. Skeat in Trengganu. There is also a paper by Mr L. Wray in no. 3 of *Perak Museum Notes* "On the Malay Method of Colouring Kris and other Blades with Arsenic," which gives an account of the chemical combinations into which the arsenic enters with the different qualities of steel and iron of which Malay kĕris-blades are composed.

[1] Though Malay smiths of former days were undoubtedly skilled in kĕris-making, probably many of the very finest blades found in the Peninsula are of Javanese, Sumatran, or Bugis origin. It is doubtful if any considerable manufacture of weapons was ever carried on in any of the west coast states, though large numbers were turned out at Trengganu, and to a less extent in Kelantan and Patani.

It is interesting to note that, in spite of the prohibition forbidding the wearing of weapons in public places, the Malay in many districts has not by any means conquered his passion for a handy weapon. The consequence of the ordinance merely is that instead of carying a *kĕris* in his waist-sash, which from its very openness promotes good behaviour and politeness, he now wears a venomous little dagger, either *tumbuk lada*, *badek* or diminutive *kĕris*, concealed beneath his clothes. These small daggers were being turned out in numbers by the smith above mentioned and his brother.

The former, a Patani[1] Malay named Awang, had set up his forge at Lenggong in Upper Perak, and in his company I spent several days in January, 1913, watching the processes described below. Before giving an account of the method of manufacture of spear and knife blades, some details of the tools used in the work may not be out of place, so as to give an idea of the very simple means by which quite complicated results are obtained. The smith's forge consists of a circular semi-open hearth of hard, dried mud, built under a slight shed. On one side of this hearth is a horizontal box-bellows of Chinese type, which is about five feet long. The blast from the bellows passes through an iron pipe in the side of the box, the outlet of which is in the centre of the hearth, a little below the level of the fire, there being a grating of iron rods covering the top of the short passage leading from the hearth centre to the entrance of the pipe, in order to prevent either of these becoming choked by ashes. The fire, the fuel for which is charcoal, is protected by mud walls about one-and-a-half feet high, except at the front and back, the former being open and the latter closed by a small sheet of iron, or an old *changkul* (native hoe) blade. The smith's tools and apparatus consist of a small anvil, made from a block of iron set in the top of a large wooden post, a couple of pairs of

---

[1] "Patani" as used in Upper Perak may connote anything coming from the Monthon Patani, known to Malays as the "*Tujoh buah nĕgri*," as the district is made up of seven small States. The Upper Perak Patani Malay is usually from Rahman or Legeh, not often from the small coastal district of Patani, to which the name is nowadays confined.

roughly-made, but effective, pincers, two hammers, one or two short cold setts, each lashed at right angles with hide or rattan binding into a wooden haft about two-and-a-half feet long, the top of which is split to receive the iron, a set of files, a pump drill with a cord of bullock hide, and a small movable vice, the last-named as well as the files being of foreign manufacture. Little gouges and chisels for cutting ornamental grooves in spear or *kĕris*-blades are also used, but are generally made as occasion requires. In addition to these the smith has a small grindstone, or emery wheel, which is fitted on one side with a wood-covered spindle. When in use, the wheel is pivoted between two upright posts and is worked by alternately pulling and releasing a cord which is wound round the spindle and attached to it at the end farthest from the stone. This operation is performed by an assistant, and the blade being ground is only applied to the stone when its revolution is away from the grinder. The specimens of work which were obtained from the smith, and are now in the Perak Museum, consist of a knife, with < shaped damascening—of the type usually called *tumbuk lada* (the pepper crusher), but by the smith *badek Patani*—a damascened spear blade, and a set of pieces illustrating the manufacture of the latter. In making the spear blade a number of pieces of iron and steel are cut and forged down until they form plates of roughly the following dimensions: length 105 mm., breadth 20 mm., thickness 3 mm. The piece selected to form the central layer of the spear is slightly thicker than the others and is of steel (*bĕsi baja*); on either side of this are placed a plate of steel (*bĕsi pĕdang*) made from an old scythe-blade, and outside each of these again a plate of *bĕsi kurai*, iron or steel of unknown composition, which the smith said he obtained from the Patani States. There are also two other plates, one on each side, composed of old Government elephant chain (*bĕsi rantai*), but these only form a guard over the damascening (*pamur*) during welding. To make the *pamur* for the particular pattern of spear chosen for the Museum, two pieces of old umbrella-rib were taken and worked into the shape shown in the plate; next two strips of *běsi pamur* (? soft wrought iron), also obtained from Patani, were bent into scrolls and hammered flat. These four pieces of metal form the *pamur*, being placed, one of each kind, outside the two plates of *běsi kurai*, with the *běsi payong* nearest the end which is to form the point of the spear. The plates of *běsi rantai* are added outside these and the whole "sandwich" is taken and carefully heated, and then dipped in a mixture of sand and water to which has been added a pinch or two of iron flakes taken from below the anvil. When the pieces have been thoroughly covered with sand, they are grasped with the pincers and again placed in the fire, which has some little time previously been sprinkled with the wet sand—the sand according to the smith acts as a flux (*pětěri*). They are next taken from the fire, beaten on the anvil, re-dipped in the sand, heated and beaten until all the layers have been welded together. The block thus formed is then further dipped, heated, and beaten on all its faces until no crevices are left, losing in the process a considerable amount of weight through scaling. When the welding has been completed to the smith's satisfaction, he takes the block and forges it out into the required shape of the spear head. Next, he slightly files the blade and rubs it with a mixture of lime juice, sulphur, and salt, in order to bring up any *pamur* which may be visible owing to the scaling away of the guard plates of *běsi rantai*. He is thus able to judge to what extent he can file up the blade without injuring the damascene. When the filing process has been completed, two ornamental grooves are cut on each side of the blade near its base, and the round ornaments below the base filed into shape. Next, the blade is heated and dipped into a mixture of buffalo fat, turtle fat and coconut oil to temper it. Then it is wiped dry and ground on the emery wheel until sufficiently polished. At this stage the damascening is invisible, or nearly so, and the blade requires to undergo a pickling and developing process in order to bring it out. With this object it is placed in a bamboo containing a mixture of lime juice, coconut milk, a little of the water used for washing rice, which has been collected from the pool of slops which is found below all Malay houses, pineapple leaves, saltpetre, pieces of *Lengkuas*[1]-stem and (?) *Gamas*-leaves. The blade is left in this mixture for a couple of nights or so, until the smith considers that the pickling or etching process is sufficiently advanced. He then cleans it in preparation for the treatment which is finally to bring up the damascening. For this he takes a small piece of red arsenic, such as is generally sold in the bazaars, half a lime, and a little juice expressed from a piece of *Lengkuas*-stem. He spreads his mat in the open, and, grasping the spear head in his left hand, exposes one face to the full light of the sun, meanwhile rubbing it lightly with the arsenic and lime juice, etc. The damascening up to this time has been very slightly visible, but after a few minutes' treatment with these materials comes into view quite clearly, much as the picture becomes visible on a photographic plate when immersed in the developer. The other face of the blade is then treated in the same way and the spear head is complete.

The use of the terms Pamur and Damascene

The term *pamur*, as used by the Malays, is not synonymous with the English word damascening. The *pamur* of a blade, strictly speaking, consists only of small ornamental pieces of metal-work applied to those surfaces of the welded block which are to become the faces of the blade. The wavy pattern along the sides of the *kĕris* or spear blade, which arises from the hammering out of the welded plates in such a way that the centre plate projects furthest at the edges and the two outer plates least, so that the edges of the plates appear in regular gradation, is by the Malays termed *kurai*. Thus in the spear head described above only the pieces of *bĕsi payong* and *bĕsi pamur* form the *pamur*, while the edges of the *bĕsi baja*, *bĕsi pedang*, and *bĕsi kurai* make up the *kurai*.

---

[1] *Lengkuas* is, according to Wilkinson, either *Alpinia conchigera* or *Alpinia galanga*.

Making the Badek Patani

In manufacturing the blade of this knife the smith first took two rods, one of *bĕsi kurai* and the other of *bĕsi baja* (steel) and welded them into a single bar. This, when complete, had a length of about one foot, and a cross section roughly of half an inch by a quarter of an inch.

The bar was then heated in the fire, seized with two pairs of pincers and given a strong right spiral twist along one-half of its length, several re-heatings being necessary before the process was complete. The other half of the bar was similarly treated, except that instead of a right it was given a left spiral twist. The portions twisted to the right and left thus met in the centre of the bar. Next, the broader sides of the bar were beaten with a hammer until the twist on them was flattened down, and then the whole bar was bent in the centre to form a U. The U was further heated and beaten until the limbs came to lie together, and had become fused. Then a piece of steel, corresponding in length to a single limb of the U—that is to say, about six inches or seven inches long and three quarters of an inch broad—was welded to the outer side of the U limb with the left spiral. This piece of steel becomes the edge of the knife, the limb with the left spiral the lower portion of the V-shaped damascening, and that with the right spiral forms the upper part of the damascene and the back of the blade. The three portions are forged into one solid block and, when complete fusion has taken place, are further hammered till they attain the shape of blade required. The methods of welding, polishing and bringing up the damascene are the same as those used for the spear head. The blade, when thus completed, has a plain undamascened edge, but the back, on either side, is composed of alternate V-shaped bands of lighter and darker metal, the damascening being further accentuated by the outer edges of the darker metal V's being inlaid with small strips of silver. The inlay is effected by cutting a groove in the iron with a small cold chisel and laying in a shred of silver; the edges of the cut left by the chisel are then hammered down until the silver is firmly gripped by them.

The Smith's charms

As in the case of most of the callings followed by Malays that of a *kĕris*-smith can boast its own peculiar set of formulae devoted to invoking the particular spirits whom the smith looks upon as the guardian genii of his trade. The two specimens given below are used in the welding of iron, but the smith also recites them at the monthly "smith's promise" (*Janji tukang*), which is sometimes called *Jĕmuan hantu* or the feeding of the spirits. Behind the smith's forge is a funnel-shaped cup, made from a rolled leaf planted in the ground; this is for holding a small offering, such as an egg or a little coconut oil. It is in and around this cup that the monthly offering is placed.

The Invocations

(1) *Bi'smi'l-lahi'r-rahmani' r-rahimi. As'salam alaikum, Tabek, Pandai Kuma, Pandai Bakar, Guru yang hormat, Guru yang harkat, walfat inna a-athaina, kul kat.*

(2) *As'salamu alaikum, Hantu Tanah, Jĕmbalang Bumi, Jin Hitam, sa-gema api, mari makan jĕmuan aku, Jin Puteh, Nur-i-Muhammad, di-dĕngar ĕngkau pĕsan aku, ĕngkau ta'-dĕngar pĕsan aku, aku sumpah, bumi sa-tapak tiada mĕnanggong, ayer sa-titek tiada bĕrjumpa, jikalau ta' lĕkat, ĕngkau tolong pĕlĕkatkan.*

These may be roughly translated as follows:

(1) In the name of God the Merciful, the Compassionate, Greetings to ye, Greeting, O Smith, Master of the Hammer, Master of the Forge, Reverenced Teacher, Famous Instructor —(Debased Arabic).

(2) Greeting to you O Spirits of the Earth and of the World and to you Black Spirit, Flame of Fire; come eat the feast I have prepared you. Hear my commands, O White Spirits, Brightness of Mohammad. If you hear them not

I curse you, may no sod of earth support your feet, no drop of water quench your thirst. If (the iron) welds not, help its welding.

These invocations, as is the case in almost all Malay spells or charms, present a curious mixture of Mohammedanism and spirit or nature worship; in many cases a leavening of Hinduism is further added.

PLATE VII

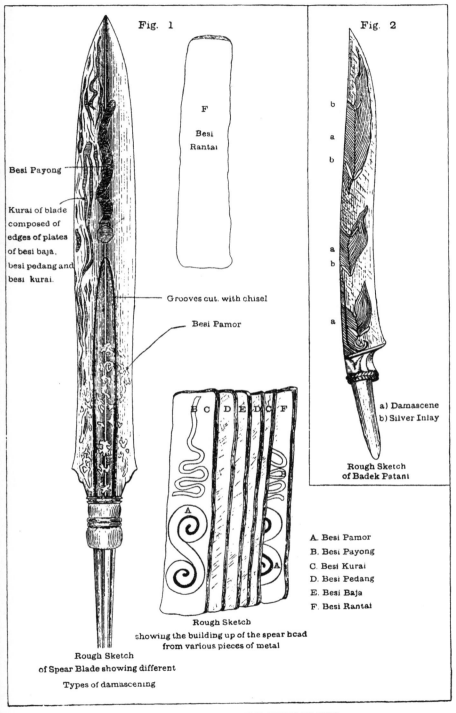

Fig. 1

Fig. 2

F
Besi
Rantai

Besi Payong

Kurai of blade
composed of
edges of plates
of besi baja,
besi pedang and
besi kurai.

Grooves cut with chisel

Besi Pamor

b
a
b

a
b

a

a) Damascene
b) Silver Inlay

**Rough Sketch
of Badek Patani**

B C D E D C F

A

A

A. Besi Pamor
B. Besi Payong
C. Besi Kurai
D. Besi Pedang
E. Besi Baja
F. Besi Rantai

**Rough Sketch
showing the building up of the spear head
from various pieces of metal**

Rough Sketch
of Spear Blade showing different
Types of damascening

DAMASCENING OF SPEAR AND KNIFE BLADES

XIII. MALAY FILIGREE WORK

By the courtesy of the Honble. Dr R. O. Winstedt, then District Officer, Kuala Pilah, I was, some years ago, enabled to visit a Malay goldsmith at the village of Berlombong, about three miles from Kuala Pilah. The art of making gold filigree was supposed to be dead in the Federated States, but Winstedt discovered several smiths in Negri Sembilan who are capable of turning out this class of work, Tukang Adam, the man visited at Berlombong, being one of them.

There is an excellent account of the manufacture of Malayan gold filigree work in Marsden's *History of Sumatra* (pp. 178–180), and this is reproduced in Winstedt's pamphlet on Malay Industries in the series of papers on Malay subjects published by the F.M.S. Government.

The present short article has little claim to add anything new to the subject, except, perhaps, the *pendinding* prayer used by the smith, but it may be useful as confirming Marsden's observations, which were made more than a hundred and thirty years ago, and showing that the same methods still prevail.

Before starting work upon the raw gold the smith repeats the following spell or prayer in order to shield himself from all harm:

Allah tuhanku, rasul Allah.
Di-hadapan aku Raja Jibrail,
Di-kiri di-kanan 'ku sĕgala sidang malaikat.
Meninding aku Salam Laut, sipat-u'llah.
Ya, Musa kalam u'llah,
Ya, hanan—ya, dayan;
Ya-sin dalam koran tiga puloh.

Oh Allah, my God; oh, prophet of God;
In front of me is prince Gabriel;
Right and left of me the whole company of angels.
My fences the Lord of the sea, the chosen (protecting) line of God.
Oh Moses, God's scribe.
Oh Merciful, Gracious.
God's word in the thirty chapters of the Koran.

Tutup terkunchi hati mulut
Barang barang satu bahaya 'kan lawan-ku;
Těrbuka, těrkěmbang sěgala pintu rězěki-ku.
Tajam měngadap aku lagi tumpul;
Bisa měngadap aku lagi tawar;
Gunching (? Kanching) pada hadap aku lagi moma (? mamah).
Aku dalam kandang kalimah.
La-ilaha-ila-lla, Muhamad rasul Allah.

Shut and locked be the hearts and the mouths
Of those who'd imperil me;
Open spread wide be the gate of mercies to me.
Let the sharp become blunt at my presence,
The venomous become robbed of its venom;
Iron bolts (?) as chewed food (?).
I stand in the fold of the faith.
There is no God but Allah and Mahommed is his Prophet[1].

The tools used by the smith are few and primitive, merely consisting of an iron plate bored with holes of different sizes, used for drawing down gold wire to the required size, three pairs of native or Chinese-made pincers, a pair of forceps, a small anvil set in a block of wood and two or three hammers of different sizes. The gold is melted in a crucible on a rectangular open hearth of earth, and the charcoal fire blown up by a horizontal box bellows[2]. A pipe from the middle of the latter leads to the hearth centre, passing under an arch of hardened clay. In addition to the open hearth, the smith uses a paraffin flare and a blowpipe for softening small pieces of gold, the flare being simply an old bottle, supported at an angle of about thirty-five degrees, with a rag stuffed into its mouth to act as a wick.

The first thing to be done in making a filigree ornament is to get ready the gold backing[3] (*tapak*) to which the fine wire patterns are to be affixed. When a sheet of gold has been cut to the size and shape required for this, the smith proceeds to draw down the wire used in making the filigree.

---

[1] I have to thank Dr Winstedt for helping me to make a correct translation of this prayer.

[2] Bamboo tubes, called *těropong*, are used in addition for blowing up the fire.

[3] Marsden calls this *papan*.

This is a long and tedious process. A piece of gold is first roughly hammered out into a wire of considerable thickness, and an end is passed through one of the largest holes in the iron plate mentioned above; the wire is then pulled through with the aid of a pair of pincers. All the holes on one side of the plate have their mouths enlarged into cup-shaped depressions of various sizes. A little coconut oil is put into the depression with a feather before the wire is drawn through the hole, and as the wire is threaded in from the side on which the depressions are, any gold which may be stripped off in the process of drawing is left behind in the cup and adheres by reason of the oil. The drawing process is repeated again and again, a smaller hole being used each time. Occasionally the wire becomes too hard to stand further fining down without breaking, and the smith then lights his paraffin flare, rolls the wire into a coil, places it on a block of charcoal and softens it by means of the flame and small brass blowpipe (*peniyup*). Each time the wire is put through a smaller sized hole the end of it has to be cut or scraped with a sharp knife, until its circumference is sufficiently small for enough of it to pass through to afford a hold for the pincers. The drawing-down process is continued—the refuse gold being occasionally scraped out from the cups and deposited in a small coconut shell plate or dish—until the wire is rather finer than an ordinary piece of sewing cotton, when it is considered ready for the next process. This consists in giving the prepared wire a twist, as Marsden observes, "like that in the handle of a whalebone punch ladle," and this is obtained by rolling the wire on a block of wood under a flat stick. When the twisting is finished, the wire is lightly tapped with a hammer until it is slightly flattened. The smith is then ready to begin composing the filigree (*karangan*; *i.e.* composition). A long piece of plain flattened wire is first taken, and a sufficient length cut from it to form a boundary round the edge of the *tapak*. This is bent into shape and fastened on edge in the required position with a kind of glue (*gĕtah kĕndĕri*), which is made from a small red seed with a black spot on it, said to

be the fruit of a climbing plant (*akar*) called *Kĕndĕri*[1]. Borax
powder (*pejar*), used as a flux, and filings from a block of
alloy of gold, silver and brass[2], are spread evenly along the
wire, which is fixed down to the backing with tiny little
clamps, made from small strips of iron, bent double. Heat
is next applied by means of the flare and blowpipe, and the
alloy, acting as a solder, fuses with the wire and the metal
of the backing. The clamps are then taken off, an inner
edging of twisted wire arranged as before, and the clamps
put back. When this has also been soldered into position in
the same manner, the clamps are finally removed, and the
smith begins the work of setting in the patterns of the
karangan. For these he bends up the twisted and flattened
wire with the forceps into the required shapes for the patterns,
cutting off each little portion of pattern as it is made. When
he has thus got enough pieces to do a large section of the work
he moistens them with the *gĕtah* to make them stick, and sets
them in position on the gold backing with the forceps. This
arrangement being finished, he covers all the *karagan* evenly
with the mixture of borax and solder, and heats it with the
blowpipe flame until the wires have become attached to the
back plate. Large pieces of the *karangan* are thus done at
one time, and when the whole of it is completed, the only
thing that remains to be done is to clean up the work. Small
round balls, called fishes' eggs (*tĕlor ikan*), made by fusing
a little gold dust on a piece of charcoal, or tiny circular gold
discs, called pepper seeds (*biji lada*), made by flattening
the aforesaid balls, are frequently applied to the filigree as
ornaments, being affixed in exactly the same way as the gold
wire. Newly made ornaments are cleaned and then (purposely) dulled, and coloured deep yellow, by letting them
simmer in a solution of alum (*tawas*), brushing them, covering
them with alum paste and putting them on a charcoal ember
for a few minutes, before brushing them again.

[1] Probably *Abrus precatorius*.
[2] The composition of this alloy is four parts gold, to one part silver and
one part brass. A small square block of the alloy is fixed into the side of
a stick of wood, which acts as a holder for it when it is being filed.

This colouring process is called *sĕpoh kuning* (yellow *sĕpoh*), as opposed to *sĕpoh merah* (red *sĕpoh*), a red colouring, much appreciated by Malays, which is frequently given to gold articles. This can be produced by two or more methods. One way, that used by Tukang Adam, is to make a solution of borax (*pijar*) and a green crystalline substance obtained from the Chinese shops which is called either *tunjong* or *gunjar*. The articles to be coloured are dipped several times alternately into the solution and into hot water, and then roasted for a short time on a charcoal ember. The result is that a dark purplish-red deposit forms all over the gold of the ornaments. In another method a mixture of saltpetre and sulphur is employed; but this was said to be troublesome to use.

The chief articles to which filigree-work is applied are the mountings of *kĕris* or dagger hilts, the tops of small boxes for holding chewing requisites, the ends (*buntut*) of *kĕris*-sheaths, rings, brooches, buttons, small clasps used instead of buttons, gold beads for threading as necklaces, ear-studs, and pendants (*dokoh*). Silver filigree work is sometimes to be obtained, that from Upper Perak and the so-called Patani States being particularly fine.

XIV. THE POTTING INDUSTRY AT KUALA TEMBELING, PAHANG

At Kuala Tembeling in Pahang a considerable potting industry is still carried on, this being one of the few stations in the Peninsula where Malays are engaged in making pottery.

An account of a similar industry on the Perak River has already been given by L. Wray (*J.R.A.I.* vol. XXXIII, p. 24 *et seqq.*) and this may be read for purposes of comparison.

The clay used by the Kuala Tembeling potters—women —is, when unbaked, of a yellow colour, and, according to my informant, is obtained from between layers of stone (*di-gali di chĕlah batu*) at a place called Pasir Durian. After excavation, it is pressed into reticulate, conical carrying-baskets (*ambong*) and conveyed, chiefly by boat, to the potters' houses. Arrived there; it is soaked in water and then placed on a slab of wood—a section of a tree-trunk— on which it is pounded with a wooden pestle until it is worked into a homogeneous mass, any impurities, such as stones or roots, being removed while it is undergoing this treatment. It is then ready for use.

No true potter's wheel is found among the Malays of the Peninsula, but a primitive substitute is made by the Tembeling people by rotating by hand a round winnowing-tray, or a flat sieve, on the above-mentioned wooden slab. A piece of coarse matting is placed in the tray and on this sufficient clay to form a pot.

Starting work in this manner, a potter, whose house I visited on two occasions, made, at my request, a specimen of the ordinary earthen cooking-bowl (*bĕlanga*). The lump of clay was quickly and cleverly worked up with the right hand until the sides and lip of the vessel had been thrown, the sieve, meanwhile, being rotated "against the clock" with the left. The only aid used was a piece of wet rag which was chiefly employed in throwing the lip of the vessel.

On reaching this stage it was necessary to stop to allow

the clay to harden somewhat, before removing the vessel from the tray, in order to give it the rounded bottom which is general in vessels of this type. The remainder of the demonstration, therefore, was postponed till the next day, when I again visited the house. The clay of the vessel had by this time become a good deal drier, but, as the potter explained, was not yet really sufficiently hard. However, as I could not pay her another visit, she said that she would do her best.

On resuming work, the pot was carefully removed from the tray, placed upside down on the potter's knee, and its base beaten into shape externally with a wooden implement (*pěněpak*), used like a bat, but shaped like a Malay working-knife.

When a sufficient degree of rotundity had been obtained, the bottom and sides of the vessel were scraped over on the outside with a knife-shaped sliver of bamboo (*pěndědak*), in order to remove superfluous clay.

The next process was the smoothing of the outer surface of the pot, and this was accomplished with the aid of a polishing-stone (*pěnggangsar*), a smooth pebble of quartz, such as may be picked up among the shingle of any Pahang river. The specimens used by potters, however, have generally attained a certain polish owing to constant use.

After this a decoration of a row of short perpendicular lines was scored on the body of the vessel below the lip, the *pěndědak* being the tool used in producing them.

This completed the treatment of the outside of the vessel, but the inside, particularly at the bottom, still remained in a rough state. In the finishing of the interior a rough circlet of brass was the chief implement used. This was like a flattened bracelet and fairly sharp at the edges. The implement, which is called *pěngukut*, was grasped firmly with the right hand so that about half of it projected beyond the knuckles, and, with the edge of this projecting portion the superfluous clay on the inside was rapidly scraped away, the action being similar to that used in scraping out the contents of a gourd. When sufficient clay had been removed, the interior was moistened with water with the hand, and finished off with the polishing-stone.

The vessel was then set aside to dry, until ready for firing. The length of time before firing takes place appears, on the average, to be about a week, but a good deal depends on the state of the weather. Pots are kept under cover while drying.

While in the neighbourhood of Kuala Tembeling, I had no opportunity of seeing pottery fired, but I understand that the vessels are heaped up, one on top of another, in a pile, and are then protected by a four-sided structure of pieces of wood placed across and across. Around this a stack of wood is built, and the whole pile ignited. The colour of the pottery, after firing, changes from yellow to red ochre.

The chief types of vessel made are the open cooking-bowl (*bĕlanga*), which sometimes has a cover, the water-gourd (*labu tanah*), the large cooking-pot (*pĕriok*) and the wide-mouthed water-vessels called *tĕrĕnang* and *buah dĕlima*, the latter being also sometimes termed *bangking*.

The water gourd is manufactured in two pieces, top and lower portion, the parts being carefully joined when the clay has dried a little.

The *pĕriok* calls for little attention. It is not ornamented.

The *tĕrĕnang* and the *buah dĕlima* are decorated with patterns made with small stamps of bamboo or wood. The *tĕrĕnang* is a storage vessel for drinking water. A small pottery plate is often used to cover its mouth and on this rests a half-coconut-shaped bowl, which is used as a drinking cup. The *buah dĕlima* fulfils the same purpose as the *tĕrĕnang*, and also frequently has the small cup and plate, as well as a saucer placed below it, but whereas the *tĕrĕnang* is a rather pot-bellied vessel with only a slight rim at its base, the *buah dĕlima* is taller, not nearly so broad, and has a well-developed foot. The name *buah dĕlima* means "pomegranate fruit," and the vessel certainly has a shape approaching that of the fruit. As is well known, and has been pointed out by L. Wray, several types of Malay vessels are derived from fruits which are still, with a little adaptation, used for the same purposes as the clay utensils. Thus the clay, or silver, drinking bowl is derived from the half coconut shell, still commonly put to this use; the clay water-bottles from two species of gourd and the larger types of water-vessel probably from the coconut shell water-pot, still commonly used. The pomegranate, however, cannot have been turned to any such use.

XV. THE MALAY FIRE-PISTON

In the collection of *Anthropological Essays Presented to Edward Burnett Tylor in Honour of his 75th Birthday* is to be found a very full and interesting paper on the fire-piston by Henry Balfour. He has demonstrated that this curious implement is known and put to practical use in the Shan States and Pegu, among the Khas and Mois, in the Malay Peninsula, in Western Sumatra, in Java (among the Sundanese and in the Kediri Residency), in Bali, Lombok, Sumbawa, Flores, parts of Borneo, and also in Mindanao and Luzon. In Europe the fire-piston seems first to have been produced in the year 1802.

The present paper is written with the object of describing certain specimens in the Perak Museum, Taiping, to which Balfour referred, but of which he had no description[1]. There are seven specimens in the Perak Museum, and three of these have been added to the collections by myself since his paper appeared[2].

The materials used in the construction of our fire-pistons are buffalo horn, wood and tin. The cylinders of the implements are all of horn or tin, the pistons sometimes of wood. I have seen the fire-piston in use on several occasions among the "Patani" Malays, who have flocked into the north of Perak from Siamese Malaya during the last hundred years or so, and, provided that the instrument is in good condition and the timber dry, can obtain fire with it myself in at least two out of three attempts. A most important part of the instrument is the binding of rag, near the distal end of the piston, which acts as a washer, and prevents the escape of air. This must be so adjusted that it allows the piston to pass smoothly down the cylinder when the piston head is given a sharp blow with the palm of the hand, and must not be so

[1] Page 30 of his paper.
[2] More have been added since this article was written, notably specimens from Chong, Trang, Peninsular Siam.

tight that there is difficulty in withdrawing the piston fairly quickly, nor so loose that air can escape from within. In museum specimens this binding, which is treated with beeswax in order to facilitate its passage, is generally out of order.

In making fire, a little piece of tinder is pushed into the depression, or cavity, at the distal end of the piston, that part of the material which is contained in the depression being fairly closely packed—to prevent it falling out—but a portion which projects beyond the piston end being left rather loose in order that it may be easily kindled by the spark. When the piston is ready, its distal end is inserted in the cylinder: the cylinder is then grasped firmly in the left hand, and the piston driven home by a sharp blow on its proximal end, extracted smartly, and the timber is found to be alight. A little experience of the instrument is necessary to get the best results, especially with regard to the withdrawal of the piston. This must be done quickly, but not roughly, or the spark will be extinguished. The following are descriptions of our specimens:

(i) Fire-piston (*gobek api*) with tin cylinder and wooden piston. Rather clumsily made. Length of cylinder 8·6 cm.; length of piston 10·1 cm. From Larut, Perak.

(ii) Fire-piston (*gobek api*) with cylinder and piston both of buffalo horn. Length of cylinder 7·6 cm.; length of piston 9·9 cm. Made at Lenggong, Upper Perak, in 1917, for I. H. N. Evans by a Malay craftsman named Ismail.

(iii) Well-made fire-piston (*gobek api*) with tin cylinder and wooden piston. Length of cylinder 9·5 cm.; length of piston 10·5 cm. Collected by L. Wray at Pulau Tiga, Lower Perak. Museum number 2135/06.

(iv) Fire-syringe (*gobek api*) with horn cylinder and wooden piston. An old specimen. Length of cylinder 7·6 cm.; length of piston 8·9 cm. Collected at Lenggong, Upper Perak, by I. H. N. Evans. Museum number 7/17.

(v) Fire-piston (*gobek api*) with both cylinder and piston of buffalo horn. A small pouch for tinder is attached by a cord to the lower end of the cylinder. Length of cylinder 8·8 cm.; length of piston 11·0 cm. Lower Perak.

(vi) Small fire-piston (cylinder and piston both of buffalo horn) with spatula and tinder-box attached to it. The tinder-box, which is made from a nut of some kind, and has a wooden stopper, is tied by a string to the base of the cylinder, while the spatula, a French nail with the point beaten out, is also attached to the same part of the instrument. The piston and the cylinder are connected by a cord. Length of cylinder 4·8 cm.; length of piston 5·5 cm. "Patani." Collected by G. F. Bozzolo.

(vii) Fire-piston (*gobek api*) with cylinder of buffalo horn and piston of wood. The specimen is remarkable for an up-turned spike proceeding from its base. This, when the instrument is held ready for use, comes up behind the fingers of the left hand. The remains of used tinder are cleaned out of the piston with the point of the spike. The top of the piston has a small hole in it, probably for containing tinder. Length of cylinder 8·4 cm.; length of piston 8·4 cm. Collected at Kampong Perak, Batu Kurau, Perak, by I. H. N. Evans in 1918. Museum number 61/18.

PLATE VIII

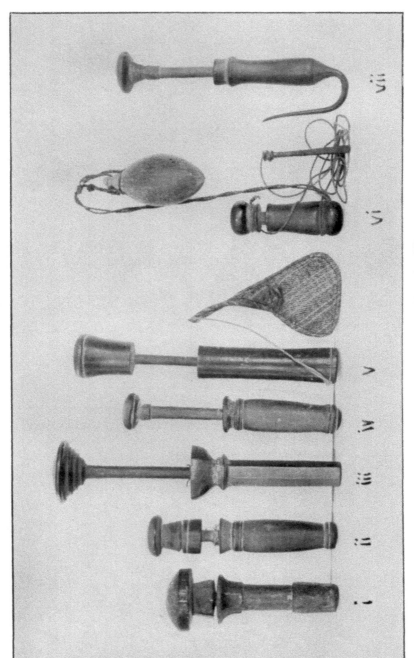

FIRE-PISTONS FROM THE MALAY PENINSULA

XVI. ON A COIN MOULD FROM KELANTAN

Through the good offices of a former British Adviser, Kelantan, the Hon. Mr H. W. Thomson, and the generosity of the Government of that State, the Perak Museum has received a very valuable addition to its collection. The donation is a two-piece mould for casting the small coins, *duit pitis*, which were, until comparatively recently, issued by the Kelantan Government.

Graham states in his book (*Kelantan*, p. 62) that "the currency chiefly in use in the bazaars and markets is a locally minted coin made from an alloy of tin and lead 'Pittis' (*sic*), a small circular coin pierced in the centre and carried in bundles threaded on a string. A bundle of fifteen coins is called a 'Keneri,' one of sixty a 'Kupang,' and four hundred and eighty 'Pittis' equal one dollar. There is at present about $160,000 worth of tin coin in circulation. The mint has been closed and it is not proposed to issue any more money of this description, as the alloy used is very soft and perishable, and the coin is easy to imitate and has been frequently counterfeited."

Graham's book was published in 1908 and his preface is dated October 5th, 1907, while Kelantan came under British control in 1909, Siam renouncing her suzerainty in favour of Great Britain in that year. Thus the issue ceased while Kelantan was still subject to Siam.

I myself visited Kota Bharu, Kelantan, early in 1921, and found *pitis* still freely current in the local market for the purchase of fish, chillies, *sireh* and other articles of small value, nine *pitis* being, according to a Malay informant, worth one cent present Straits Settlements currency (1 ct.= 2s. 4d. ÷ 100). Inche Wan Lela, Penghulu of Kuala Lipis, Pahang, to whom I have translated Graham's account, confirms its general correctness and says that, at the time that he visited Kelantan, four hundred and eighty *pitis* were equal to one "cannon dollar" (a Spanish coin), while the Mexican dollar was worth only four hundred and forty.

As will be seen from the illustration which accompanies this paper, fifteen *pitis* are cast at one pouring, a central channel in each side of the mould giving rise to fourteen side branches, seven on each side, each of which terminates in a mould for one side of a *pitis*, while the main channel gradually narrows and ends in two similar half-moulds. The *pitis*, therefore, when taken from the mould, are connected by twigs of metal to a main stem[1]. These are, of course, subsequently cut away.

The two pieces of the mould are of brass and of considerable weight and thickness. On the inner face of one section are four pegs—one towards each corner—and the other has four holes in corresponding positions. The object of these is to ensure correct register when the mould is in use. Each section also has four holes in it at the sides, being, presumably, for the insertion of cramps. As the *pitis* are cast with holes in them, it is necessary that there should be projections in the centres of the coin moulds in order to prevent the molten metal from filling this part. This is effected, not by pins projecting from one side of each mould only, but by stumpy projections on both sides, which meet, or almost meet, when the two halves of the mould are placed in conjunction. These projections, however, have holes in them, and wooden, or iron, pegs were, perhaps, inserted in these to help in obtaining a more correct register, though it appears that, on the (?) last occasion that the mould was used, these pegs were not in place, for several of the holes, owing to leakage between the projections, are filled with the metal from which the *pitis* were made.

The inscriptions on the *pitis* cast in this mould are the same on both sides of the coin. They are in Arabic and a translation of them which I have had made reads, "Struck on the 5th of (the month) Dzu'l-hijjah, 1321" (A.H.).

---

[1] In *Hobson Jobson*, under the heading "Pagoda-tree," will be found an interesting, but I should think incorrect, suggestion that the idea of a tree bearing coins may have been derived from some such currency as that of Kelantan.

PLATE IX

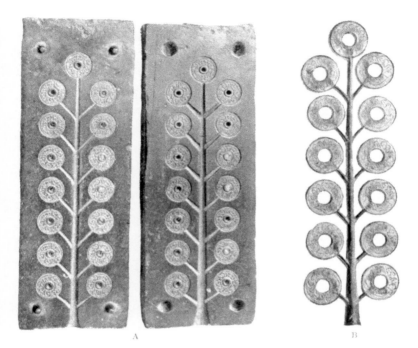

COIN-MOULD FROM KELANTAN AND "TREE" OF COINS

A Two halves of mould for *pitis*. Measurements of one side 25·1 × 9·2 ×
    2·5 cm.

B "Tree" of *pitis* with date 1314 (A.H.). These coins are larger than the
    pitis of the mould. Both photographs were taken at practically the
    same distance.

XVII. NAKON NIELLO-WARE

While travelling in Peninsular Siam, in 1924, I stopped for a few days at Nakon Sritamarat to inquire into the method of manufacturing the celebrated niello-ware, which is known in the Malay States as *chutam*.

My first visit was to the Nakon Art School, where I found several pupils engaged in making sets of niello-ware coat-buttons. A stamp of the pattern to be produced on the button is first printed with ink on to a piece of thin paper. This is next affixed to a flat piece of silver on which the shape of the button-face had been traced with a graving-tool, and the disc so marked cut out. The background of the pattern, which is to be filled in with enamel, is then punched down, leaving the design standing out in low relief. Next the silver disc is made convex on one surface, concave on the other, being placed in a brass die and struck with the rounded end of an iron bar. After this the convex surface is covered with the black enamel substance in coarsely powdered form, this being mixed with a saturated solution of borax, which, I take it, acts as a flux. The button is then grasped with a pair of tongs and turned about in the flame of a charcoal fire, which is blown upon by a box bellows, until the enamel fuses. Superfluous enamel is next removed with a file and a graving-tool, and the surface further cleaned with sand- and emery-paper. A final polishing is given with crocus-powder, and the button, with the exception of its shank, is complete.

As only small articles in niello-ware are usually made in the Art School, and as I could not get a detailed account of the manufacture of the enamel substance there, since they purchased their supplies from outside, I made arrangements to visit the house of a Siamese craftsman to obtain more ample information. Accompanied by a locally born Malay, I made my way to a village close to the gaol, and here we found the smith at home.

The following is his receipt for the enamel:

Take of lead seven ticals twenty-five satangs' weight.
Take of sulphur one kattie.
Take of copper five ticals weight.
Take of silver one tical seventy-five satangs' weight.

The lead, copper and silver are to be weighed with modern Siamese silver coinage.

First heat the copper, lead and sulphur together and allow the mixture to cool. Next heat again and add the silver. The enamel is then, in its rough state, a hard, black, shiny substance, something like slag in appearance. It requires to be powdered before use.

In addition to obtaining the above receipt, I was also able to observe the smith—a master of his craft—at work on the finest *chutam* bowl that I have ever seen. I tried to purchase this but, unluckily, it had been ordered by a Siamese nobleman of Singgora. When I arrived, I found that the designs to be reproduced were being applied to the bowl in truncated wedge-shaped sections, running from top to bottom, and with the narrower, and truncated, parts of the wedges directed downwards. The method is first to whiten such a section of the outside of the bowl with the rice-starch powder that is ordinarily used by Siamese and Malay women for cosmetic purposes. The designs are then scratched upon this white surface, and the background punched down, or cut away, until the patterns stand out in relief. This part of the bowl is next smoked, and a print of the design taken on moistened tissue-paper. The piece of paper, thus printed, is cut to shape and stuck upon a fresh section of the bowl, and the background dealt with as in the first panel, the process being repeated until the bowl is completely covered with patterns.

Though I did not see the enamel substance applied by the silversmith, the method appears to be the same as that employed at the Nakon Art School in the case of the buttons. He informed me that the best gilding of the patterns, in pieces which are so treated, is done with gold leaf, which adheres readily, but is burnt in before the bowl undergoes a final polishing.

At the Art School, in order to demonstrate the tenacity of the enamel, one of the instructors took a *chutam* button and twisted it badly out of shape with two pairs of pliers. On examining it after this rough treatment, it was found that the enamel had neither flaked nor cracked, but had followed the twistings and bendings to which the button had been subjected.

PART IV

ARCHAEOLOGY

XVIII. A GRAVE AND MEGALITHS IN NEGRI SEMBILAN

THE ancient monuments at Pengkalan Kempas, Linggi, Negri Sembilan, collectively called Kĕramat Sungai Udang, have been known to Europeans for a considerable time, though I believe that no detailed description of them has yet been published. They stand in a small valley or depression between two ridges, and only a few chains distant from the Sungai Udang (Prawn River).

The local Malays are full of stories about the monuments, but, on questioning the older men, it is found that the truth is that they were discovered in the jungle only some two or three generations ago, and that the stories are therefore of quite recent date. Nowadays the jungle has disappeared and the small reserve, in which the remains are enclosed, is surrounded by Chinese and Malay rubber holdings.

The work of excavating and restoring the monuments as far as possible, some of which had suffered from ill-treatment, accidental or otherwise; from natural decay; or had fallen down owing to subsidence of the soil, was begun by me towards the end of July, and finished about the middle of October, 1919. After some clearing work had been done, but before any of the stones had been moved or excavations proper begun, a survey of the whole site was made by Mr W. A. Wallace of the Federated Malay States Surveys and, with his kind permission, I publish one of the plans that he made (Plate XVI).*

The chief remains at Kĕramat Sungai Udang are a Mohammedan tomb with an inscribed pillar, and a group of carved granite monoliths with a platform in front of them. The

*This plate is now available for download from
www.cambridge.org/9781107600652

Mohammedan tomb is, in some ways, the less interesting of the structures as it is possible to date it accurately; the granite monoliths the more interesting since their age is problematical.

The grave is an object of veneration both to Malays and Chinese, and to a certain extent to Tamils. The Malays and Chinese make and pay vows there; the former holding feasts (*kĕnduri*), at which *pulut kunyet*[1] figures prominently, whenever the *Dato'* of the *Kĕramat*[2] has granted their requests; the latter firing crackers, making offerings of fowls—subsequently taken away for consumption at home—and of spirituous liquors, of which the Mohammedan *Dato'* surely cannot approve, and being only restrained from offering pork by the interdiction of the local Malays; furthermore they defile the monument by burning candles, joss-sticks and "paper money"—the variety with which the Chinese placate spirits and the ghosts of the departed—in every available crack and crevice. The grave has been protected for many years by a palm-leaf roof.

To return however to the granite monoliths: the main group of these consists of three uprights[3] with three dressed blocks of laterite[4] placed on the ground in front of them. The uprights have been given fanciful names by the Malays: one, a long, tapering, sculptured flake of granite is said to be the sword (*Pĕdang*) or *Kĕris* of the Saint of the *Kĕramat*, the second his spoon (*Sudu*), and the third the rudder (*Kĕmudi*) of the ship in which he arrived in the country. In addition to these there is also a large turtle-back of granite[5] lying rather to one side, and two smaller granite uprights (nos. 103 and 104), one of which may perhaps have been roughly dressed. The *Sudu* (nos. 93 and 101 in plan) was broken into two pieces some years ago by a falling tree. I was able, however, to make a fairly good restoration of the stone. The same cause, too, was probably responsible for the fracture

---

[1] Glutinous rice dyed with turmeric.
[2] "Grandfather" of the sacred place.
[3] Nos. 92, 101 and 93, 94, in Mr Wallace's plan.
[4] Nos. 98, 99, 100 in plan.   [5] No. 102.

of a small granite monolith which originally stood within the outermost course of stones surrounding the grave. The base of this was discovered buried in its original position[1], and the larger portion of the stone has now been joined to it and erected as it originally stood.

The turtle-back (no. 102), to which I have referred above, was found lying, flat side up, as shown in the plan, but I turned it over and had it placed as nearly as possible in the position in which it had formerly been, to one side of, and rather behind the *Kĕmudi* (no. 94), as shown in a photograph taken some years previous to my visit.

The blocks forming the platform in front of the three main uprights are all of laterite, and number three, not four, as in the plan. The inaccuracy is due to the fact that one of them (no. 100) had been much broken, and looked, in the state in which it was found, as if it was really two distinct blocks. Mr Wallace indicated, however, that he was not sure of the number and form of the blocks of part of the platform by means of dotted lines. The shapes of several of the stones comprising the group are, to say the least of it, remarkable and it seems possible that the *Kĕris* (no. 92) may be a conventionalized *phallus*, while the *Sudu* (nos. 93 and 101) may, perhaps, be a representation of the *yoni*.

Of the platform blocks two are rectangular (nos. 99 and 100), one being almost square; the third block is a rough hexagon. It is worthy of note that several of the granite monoliths show notchings, ribbings, or crenulations at their edges, nos. 92 and 94 affording good examples of ribbing, while the turtle-back (no. 102) is crenulate at one edge.

The sculptured designs which stand out in somewhat low relief on the *Kĕmudi* (no. 94) and the *Pĕdang* (no. 92) are extremely interesting. Those on the former appear to be chiefly zoomorphic grotesques. At the bottom of the designs on the *Kĕmudi* can be distinguished an animal which appears to be meant for a horse or pony, while just above it is another zoomorph, seemingly a bird, the legs of which are, however,

[1] Close to No. 144, also a granite monolith.

prolonged, one passing downwards and bending under the feet of the "horse" to end finally in a club-shaped appendage behind that animal's tail, the other curving upwards to form a similar club-shaped object behind the "bird's" body. It seems not impossible that the bird may be a crude representation of a peacock since the head bears a projection which is, perhaps, the peacock's crest, while the club-shaped appendage behind it may be meant for its tail. The discoidal object, too, in the centre of the stone is extremely interesting as it may possibly show that the constructors of the monument were sun-worshippers or moon-worshippers[1].

The rest of the designs in relief may be, as I am inclined to think that they are, highly conventionalized plumes of feathers, or possibly phyllomorphic grotesques.

I have yet omitted to mention the very curious projection on the left of the stone; this appears to be the conventionalized head of an animal of some kind. The curly barbule under the chin is a most peculiar feature of the sculpture.

To pass now to the *Pĕdang* (no. 92). There can, I think, be no doubt at all that the lowest object represented on this is a dragon. The body, tail, head, and recurved horns are all distinctly marked, and the snout of the animal projects between the ribbings at the edge of the stone.

The other sculptured objects on the stone are much more problematical; that directly above the dragon is, I am pretty sure, an animal grotesque of some kind: looked at in one light it appears to be a buffalo's head with ears, nose, eyes and mouth fairly plainly defined; in another, part of it appears to represent a bird with outspread wings, recurved and retracted legs, and a long tail bent somewhat to one side[2]. Above this carving are representations of three discoidal

[1] Mr E. E. W. G. Schröder tells me that he considers that the stone monuments of Nias are connected with moon-worship, not with sun-worship.

[2] Dr Bosch, Director of the Antiquarian Survey of the Dutch East Indies, to whom I have shown a photograph of the *Pĕdang*, thinks that this peculiar carving may be a degenerate representation of the head of the *Kala* (a mythical animal) which is frequently found depicted on Javanese ruins of the Hindu period.

objects, set triangularly, the uppermost being a plain disc, like that on the *Kĕmudi*, to which I have already referred. The lower two, which form a pair, have each a curved line running from their outer edges to near their centres. Next above the uppermost disc comes a bowed dividing ridge in relief, and above this again the word "Allah" in Arabic character, and standing out in relief. After this the stone tapers to its curiously shaped head, which can be well seen in the illustration.

I have already put forward, with some diffidence, the view that the *Pĕdang* may be a conventionalized *phallus*. If this is so, I would suggest that the portion of the stone above the inscription represents the *glans*, while the band, to which I have just referred, may be meant to represent the scar left by circumcision[1]. The whole group of stones, apart of course from the inscription, is absolutely foreign in design and spirit to the custom and teaching of Islam and there would appear to be fairly good reasons for considering the granite monoliths to be of older date than the Mohammedan grave, and possibly antecedent to the propagation of Islam in the Malay Peninsula. Only subsidiary stones to the granite monoliths are of laterite while, in the case of the Mohammedan grave, laterite, with the exception of four stones of *batu Acheh* (a kind of sandstone brought from Achin), is the only material of the dressed blocks of which the structure is built. Furthermore, two small granite monoliths, obviously unconnected with the grave, stand within the quadrangle of the outermost wall of laterite blocks, and two others[2] just outside the aforesaid wall near one corner. Moreover, one piece of granite, taken from the "older" remains, was discovered in the foundations of the outer wall on its downhill side; and another, a discoidal granite flake, presumably dressed at the edges, while excavating the wall between the central block of the grave and the outer course or wall. I think, therefore, that the probabilities

---

[1] There is reason for thinking that a form of circumcision may have been practised in the Peninsula before the advent of Mohammedanism.

[2] No. 107 and another stone not shown in the plan.

are that the builders of the Mohammedan tomb found the granite monoliths already in position—probably they were regarded with a considerable degree of reverence—and left them, in so far as possible, undisturbed even where they occurred on the site marked out for the tomb. A few pieces of granite—perhaps mere waste stuff from the construction of the granite monuments—were however used in making the foundations of it.

If the above assumptions are correct, we have still to account for the name of God which is carved upon the *Pĕdang*. It is extremely unlikely that the Arabic script or the Arabic word for God arrived in the Peninsula prior to the propagation of Mohammedanism. I would suggest, therefore, that the builders of the tomb, followers of the Prophet, made a compromise between their Islamic dislike of pagan monuments and sculptures and their native fear of, and reverence for, pre-Mohammedan holy places, and that they carved the word "Allah" on the *Pĕdang*, in order to sanctify an infidel monument, for which, in spite of their religion, they, or the then inhabitants of the district, had still a considerable regard. This, at any rate, is the view taken by Wilkinson[1].

The Mohammedanism of the Malays of the Peninsula at the present day is often but a thin veneer over older strata of Hinduism and animism, and it is common to find sacred spots, especially under large trees or near caves, which are obviously the holy places of animism, and not of Islam; but which, to get round a difficulty, are sometimes said to be

---

[1] *Papers on Malay Subjects, Malay History*, p. 7. I certainly do not think that the inscription on the perforated pillar was ever changed, as Wilkinson suggests. This pillar belongs to the Mohammedan grave, and an orthodox Mohammedan inscription surely might well be expected to be found upon it.

Another point which may be mentioned here is that Wilkinson says that "it is believed that this pillar (which has been much used for oaths and ordeals) will tighten round the arm of any man who is rash enough to swear falsely when in its power." I was not told anything about false oaths by the Malays, but was informed that the stone would retain the hand and arm of any person who had not been born in lawful wedlock. Several Malays whom I met at the *kĕramat* were afraid to insert their hands in the hole.

kĕramat Jin—I presume *Jin Islam, i.e.* Mohammedan *Jin*[1]—
in order to bestow some slight appearance of orthodoxy upon
those who make, or pay, vows at them.

Similar instances of pagan sacred wells having been annexed
by the early Christians and credited to some saint are, of
course, well known in Europe.

What I have written above is one method of solving the
problem, and the arguments for the inscription having been
added to a pre-Mohammedan monument at a later date seem
to me to be strengthened by the occurrence of granite monuments within the space occupied by the Mohammedan tomb.

Of other possible explanations there are two; one of these
being that the granite monuments and the tomb are contemporaneous[2] and that the ornamentation of the former
was produced when the people had been scarcely weaned at
all (by Mohammedan missionaries) from the most pagan
practices. In this case, of course, the word "Allah" would
have been carved by the makers of the granite monoliths,
and it must in fairness be said that an inspection of the
characters, which stand out in relief, does not, to my mind,
furnish any proof that it is not contemporaneous with the
designs on the stone.

In order to make it of later date than the carvings it is
necessary to imagine that the part of the stone now occupied
by the name of God formerly stood at a higher level than
the ribbings which fringe the edges of the stone, and that this,
except for the lettering, was subsequently cut away to its
present level. The explanation is not very satisfactory, for,
as I have mentioned above, the inscription shows no signs
of having been added afterwards.

[1] There are said to be both *Jin Islam* and *Jin Kafir, i.e.* Mohammedan
and heathen Jin.

[2] This is the view taken by R. O. Winstedt (*Journ. Straits Branch Roy.
Asiat. Soc.* 1917, p. 173). He thinks it "possible that parts of the Saint's
tomb were constructed locally, and that other parts, like the ornate so-
called "sword," were brought from India, as we have seen was a common
custom." It seems to me, however, that it is much more likely that the
"sword," which is of granite containing large crystals of felspar, a type of
rock found in the peninsula, was made locally. The sandstone of the pillar
(*batu Acheh*) is, I believe, not found in the country

The third possibility—also not very satisfying—is that the granite monuments are older than the grave, but not older than the introduction of the religion of Islam into the Peninsula, and that the word "Allah" was carved upon the stone, at the same time as the other ornamentation, by a people who, though nominally Mohammedans, were, in fact, still pagan at heart[1]. The period, however, between the conversion of the first Moslem king of Malacca and the reign of Sultan Mansur Shah, in whose time the Mohammedan tomb was erected, is not long. Sultan Mohammed Shah, the first sovereign of Malacca to accept Mohammedanism, ascended the throne somewhat before the year A.D. 1403, and was recognized by the Chinese Emperor in A.D. 1405. Sultan Mansur Shah came to the throne about A.D. 1459[2]. How long the Malays in general, if they did so, had accepted Mohammedanism before the conversion of Sultan Mansur Shah, it seems impossible to say.

Of the other granite monuments yet undescribed, the most remarkable are probably a large flat and almost circular object (no. 95) which is sometimes called the Saint's Shield (*Pĕrisai*) and a small group of stones at the extreme edge of the *Kĕramat* reserve, where it now abuts on a Chinese rubber plantation. The *Pĕrisai* is chiefly noteworthy for the geometric designs in low relief on one surface. The top of the stone is marked by a small somewhat stalk-like projection; below this comes a pattern which is common in Malay designs, and the rest of the face of the stone is, as may be seen in the illustration, ornamented with the type of design already alluded to.

The group of stones near the Chinese rubber plantation, when found, was in a very ruinous condition. The most important members of it are a long flake of granite, a squared block of laterite and a round stone, also of laterite. The granite flake had, as I was told by the local residents,

---

[1] Thus we might account both for the name of God and the carvings on the *Pĕdang* appearing to be of the same date, and also for the occurrence of unrelated granite stones within the enclosure of the Mohammedan tomb.

[2] *Papers on Malay Subjects, Malay History*, pp. 22 and 24.

originally stood upright between the two laterite stones and, when we discovered it, though fallen down, one end was still resting between them. It appears that this monument, also, had been broken by a falling tree, but further damage had been done subsequently by a Chinese washerman who had broken off pieces from the upper end of the granite flake, and used them for supports for his cauldron. The Malays told me, with considerable glee, that the offender's wife had died not long afterwards, and that the washerman himself had encountered other misfortunes—all of which they ascribed to his sacrilegious act—and finally had run away. At the time of my visit, however, a brother tradesman had taken his place, and was still using the old stand for his cauldron.

Having persuaded this man to move his pitch, we discovered several pieces of the granite monolith on the site of his operations, but, unfortunately, some of them had become friable and lost their original edges owing to the constant heating which they had undergone. Nevertheless, we were lucky enough to find the top of the monolith, and to be able to establish a join with the major portion.

Partly below the squared laterite block, already mentioned, is another seemingly undressed slab of the same material, the two blocks thus forming a couple of steps.

The round laterite stone has a curious somewhat horse-shoe-shaped object sculptured on it in relief; the convex side of the granite upright, too, appears to have had a similar design depicted upon it, but it is much weathered. These two objects are particularly interesting in view of the possible phallic origin of the *Pědang*. It is possible, moreover, that, judging by its shape, the granite upright of this small group may also be meant for a rude representation of a phallus.

Of the yet undescribed granite objects there remain only a few to be dealt with. Three of these are loose and have no certain location, but I found them lying in front of the Mohammedan grave. What any of them represent it is extremely difficult to say, though they have all three been shaped, and in the case of two a little carving has been added, on one in the shape of some notchings and a slight design of patterns, on the other notchings only.

I have already referred to a small granite monolith, which had been broken, but of which we found the base while excavating the walk round the grave, which is bounded by the outermost row of stones[1]. This, like several of the other stones, is crenulate at the edges and has, furthermore, a couple of small spur-like projections, one on either side. In addition to this, standing near it, is a somewhat larger monolith (no. 44), also with crenulate edges and having some slight scrollings on one side, these being in connection with the crenulations. The two monuments appear to have been left undisturbed by the builders of the Mohammedan tomb.

Outside the course of stones which bounds the grave are a few other, mostly rather unimportant, dressed, or dressed and carved, granite stones. Only one of these, a plain and short dressed post of stone (no. 107), is shown on the plan, but there is also a small, somewhat shield-shaped upright adjacent to it, and about in front of stone no. 75. Outside the outer course of the tomb, too, and just outside block no. 77 we found a curiously carved stone, which looks almost as if it may be a conventional representation of a turtle.

To turn now to the excavation which I made, and the restorations that I attempted in connection with the granite monoliths.

The most important piece of work was the treatment of the group of stones comprising the *Pĕdang* (or *Kĕris*), the *Sudu*, the *Kĕmudi* and other elements. I have already remarked that all the monuments stand in a sort of little valley, or depression between two ridges. The large group of granite monoliths, being nearer to the middle line of the valley than the Mohammedan tomb, is on swampy ground, while the tomb is kept dry by the fact that it rests partly on the foot of the adjacent ridge, partly on artificially banked-up ground.

When I arrived at Pĕngkalan Kĕmpas, I found that, with the exception of the few granite objects in the immediate

[1] Page 83.

vicinity of the tomb and the small group near the rubber plantation, all the granite monuments had been overwhelmed by scrubby jungle and undergrowth, the land on which they stood being either actually under water, or very swampy. The first steps, therefore, were to clear away the jungle undergrowth and to put in ditches to carry off the water.

The clearing of the ground took several days, and some difficulty was encountered in dealing with a patch of *asam kělubi* (*Zalacca conferta*), the thorns of which caused the coolies much annoyance by constantly getting into their hands and feet, while a large banyan-tree, the roots of which had split the block of laterite forming the platform in front of the *Pědang* and had even penetrated the centre of the Mohammedan tomb, also gave us considerable trouble.

Having cleared the ground, I found a small and almost choked watercourse running along the bottom of the little valley, so I had a temporary ditch, which we afterwards replaced by a properly graded larger one, put in along this line to carry off some of the water. When this had been done, I had two tributary ditches driven from near the side of the tomb to the main ditch, so as to enclose the *Pědang* and the other large monoliths of the group between them. Next, the ground having become sufficiently dry, the soil surrounding the monoliths was excavated, so as to leave them standing on only a small island. The material thus removed consisted of about a foot of humus followed by rather more than the same amount of white sand, under which again was a more or less peaty stratum, about five or six inches deep, which contained twigs, leaves and branches of trees. This peaty layer was in turn succeeded by a dark greyish clay.

When overhead tackle had been got into position for lifting the monoliths, so that they might be placed on a cement raft, I decided to do the work bit by bit and to deal with the lower part of the *Sudu*[1] first. Having secured it firmly, ready for hoisting, I had the surrounding soil cleared away and

---

[1] The top part, it will be remembered, had been broken off. There were thus two portions (nos. 93 and 101).

found that its lower end was sunk in the ground to a depth of two feet only. The base of the *Pědang* proved to be even less deeply embedded as it only reached a depth of one-and-a-half feet.

As these two monoliths were the most deeply set in the ground of any, we may take them into consideration when determining the horizon of the land surface at the time when these monuments were erected. I have remarked that the present accumulation of humus with the white sand amounts to a little over two feet while the bases of none of the monuments reach a greater depth than this. I am inclined to think that the top of the white sand was probably the surface of the soil at the time when the megaliths were set up, unless some intervening layers were denuded in the period, if any, between the construction of the megalithic group and the deposition of the present humus.

The view that the layer of sand, or the top of it, was the ancient land surface is supported by the fact that it contains numerous small fragments of charcoal, and in it were found the only objects of interest that we discovered while making our excavation around the group of monoliths.

These comprised four small button-shaped objects of blue glass—one of them opaque, the other three transparent—a piece of greenish-grey céladon-ware, slightly ribbed on its convex or outer side, which looks as if it had been a part of a cup[1]; and a lid, somewhat like that of a small teapot, of which the decoration is in under-glaze painting in a dark blackish-blue on a white surface. The designs are a set of six alternating sepals around the small knob at top of the lid, and a sort of debased key-pattern near the edge. This piece of pottery is obviously Chinese. Another interesting specimen which was found is a little oval black stone of a similar nature to that which was formerly used for making stone implements. This is convex above, probably partly

---

[1] This grey ware, according to the late Sir Hercules Read, who inspected some of the fragments of pottery, may, perhaps, have been made at Sawankalok in Siam.

naturally rounded by river action, but has been artificially flattened by rubbing below. I would suggest that this was used either as a sharpening-stone for small metal tools, or as a touchstone.

Before I deal in detail with the re-erection of the monoliths and the measures taken to preserve them, or make any observations connected with their signification and, if possible, former use, I may as well refer here to the other objects found during our excavations, except those which can be definitely connected with the Mohammedan tomb.

One or two objects were discovered when making the ditch down the centre of the valley; they comprise some pieces of very rough pottery—not Chinese—which contain much grit, owing presumably to the clay of which they were made being of bad quality and never having been cleaned. Their colour is grey with occasional red streaks. The other objects found in this ditch were the remains of three posts still *in situ*, their ends, which had been sharpened and hardened by burning, being embedded in soil three-and-a-half feet below present ground level.

In a tributary to the main ditch, which was dug in order to drain some of the marshy land towards the southern end of the *Kĕramat* reserve, we came across a few other interesting objects, a small silver coin[1], two small pieces of a céladon bowl, the lower part of a small blue-and-white dish, and portions of two blue-and-white cups or small bowls. All this pottery was obviously Chinese, the blue-and-white ware, and probably the céladon as well, being of the Ming period. The céladon-ware is remarkable for its beauty. The glaze is a translucent apple-green and is crackled, while the body of the vessel has been decorated with incised foliate designs before the application of the glaze[2].

I have yet omitted to mention that while making excavations near the small group of monoliths at the edge of the

[1] This is very much rubbed, and though remains of an inscription can be seen, it will probably be impossible to identify it.

[2] Sir Hercules Read believed this green céladon-ware to be of the early Ming period (fourteenth or fifteenth century).

Chinese rubber plantation, we encountered the end of another post, and a piece of greyish-green crackled céladon was discovered built into the foundations for the washerman's copper. To proceed now to the description of the reconstructional work done:

The group of stones containing the *Kĕmudi*, the *Pĕdang* and the *Sudu* was placed on a concrete raft. Few changes were made in the position of the stones: the *Kĕmudi* was raised from its recumbent position and set at right angles to the line formed by the *Pĕdang* and the *Sudu*, this being, as far as it is possible to tell, as it stood originally; while the turtle-back (no. 102), which was found lying flat side uppermost, was turned over and placed in position somewhat behind the *Kĕmudi*. These, with the exception of planting the *Pĕdang* perpendicularly, which was leaning at an angle, and a slight straightening up of stones nos. 92 and 104, were the only changes made.

Excavation of the site revealed four large undressed blocks of laterite underlying the largest stone of the platform, that in front of the *Pĕdang*, and smaller blocks under stones nos. 99 and 98. These were replaced as found. Furthermore, pieces of laterite, seemingly placed there with a view to keeping the large perpendicular megaliths in position, were found behind the bases of the *Pĕdang*, the *Sudu* and the *Kĕmudi*[1].

With regard to the small group of stones near the boundary of the Chinese rubber plantation, these objects were placed on a concrete platform. The granite flake, which had fallen over, was set up perpendicularly, and such pieces of its upper end as we could fit re-joined to it. Luckily the top of the flake was found near the washerman's cauldron, and a join secured, though some portions of the stone were not discovered, this necessitating a somewhat free use of cement, so as to secure the monument against damage in the future.

In addition to the stones already described, three outlying

---

[1] Probably these stones were added recently by a former member of the F.M.S. Museums' Staff. They are quite small.

blocks of granite were discovered by sounding the ground with an iron rod, and also a small heap of material, laterite and granite pieces. The three blocks just referred to were natural boulders of granite, while the heap of stones contained a piece of granite which had apparently been a part of some monument, since some carving in relief—though it was not possible to identify the object depicted—could be discerned on it.

To turn now to the Mohammedan tomb. This consists of an outer course of squared stones surrounding an inner structure built of much larger blocks of the same material[1]. At one end, between the outer wall or course and the inner block, is a squared pillar of sandstone (*batu Acheh*) which has a hole through it and bears on its four faces four inscriptions, two in Arabic character, two in some script which is now said to be old Javanese. The two inscriptions in "Javanese" are shorter than those in the Arabic lettering and fill the spaces, one on either side, above the two openings of the hole[2].

The Arabic inscriptions, except for an orthodox Mohammedan invocation at the beginning of each, are difficult to read; but it appears to be clear from those parts of them which it has been possible to decipher that the tomb is that of one Sheikh Ahmad[3] who died in A.H. 872 (A.D. 1467/8) in the time of Sultan Mansur Shah of Malacca[4] (A.D. 1459–1475)[5]. Malacca was taken by the Portuguese under Albuquerque in A.D. 1511, in the reign of Sultan Mahmud Shah, and

[1] Mention may here be made of a curious little platform, consisting of two blocks of laterite, which projects from the outer course of stones on the side facing the *Sudu*. The larger stone of this platform (no. 96) rests on a cylindrical pillow stone of the same material.

[2] Since the above was written Dr P. V. van Stein Callenfels has read nearly all of the inscriptions in old Javanese character. He finds it recorded, in Malay much mixed with Javanese words, that "Ahmad Majanu" came down stream "to play a trick" and was killed with his children and army.

[3] "*Makam Sheikh Ahmad*" (the tomb of Sheikh Ahmad).

[4] "*Pada zaman Sultan Shah Mansur*" (in the time of Sultan Mansur Shah). My thanks are due to Mr J. P. Moquette of the Batavian Society's Museum for making out a large part.

[5] R. O. Winstedt, *tom. cit. supra*, p. 172.

between Sultan Mansur Shah and Sultan Mahmud Shah came Alaedin Riayat Shah I.

I have already referred to the inner part of the tomb. This, as will be seen on referring to the plan, consists of an outer and an inner enclosure, both of them rectangular, and both constructed of very large and heavy blocks of laterite. The inner chamber is the grave proper, and at its foot there is a capstone[1] of *batu Acheh* (no. 2) above a laterite block, which on its outer face has an Arabic inscription within a circle. This is much worn and I have, as yet, been able to read nothing, though it is said that a date was to be deciphered on it not many years ago.

At the head of the grave there is a laterite block (no. 3) the top of which has been rounded to resemble the *batu Acheh* capstone referred to above. This stone also bears a circle on its outer, and another on its inner, surface, these corresponding in position to those on the capstone. Neither of them now contains any inscription.

Spanning the space between the inner and outer walls of the central block of the tomb, on its two longer sides, are six remarkable stones, three on each side. There are two pairs of uprights (nos. 4, 5, 6 and 7) and two blocks which lie between them (nos. 13 and 18). The two pairs of uprights differ somewhat in shape and size, and there are some slight differences between the two horizontal blocks (nos. 13 and 18), one of them being rectangular in section and having a vertical band in relief, about four inches wide, running from top to bottom in the middle on its inner side, while the other stone has its lower inner edge trimmed away, and a horizontal band in relief on its inner side which divides the stone into about two equal portions, a vertical band of the same size running from the centre of the top edge of the stone to join the horizontal band, but not being continued below it.

[1] Presumably this is an inscribed stone to which Wilkinson refers in his *Malay History*. He says, "Near this pillar (*i.e.* the perforated stone) is another cut stone on which the lettering of some old non-Arabic inscription can be dimly seen," but as far as I have been able to make out the inscription seems to be undoubtedly in the Arabic character.

I will now describe the reconstructional work done and refer to certain interesting objects which were found in the course of the excavations:

The grave is built at the foot of a small hill, one of its longer sides lying towards the swampy ground which I have mentioned previously. The first step taken was to clear away the earth round the outer edging of stones. On this being done, it was found that the edge of the structure consisted of two courses of squared laterite blocks, one superimposed on the other, the blocks of the lower layer being the larger. On the side directly below the hill, and at the two ends of the structure, this outer wall was reinforced by a row of laterite boulders placed exteriorly against the lower course of stones, and against the earth which supported it. This feature was very much more marked on the side facing the swamp. Here the lower course of stones and the earth below it had been banked up with very large boulders thus:

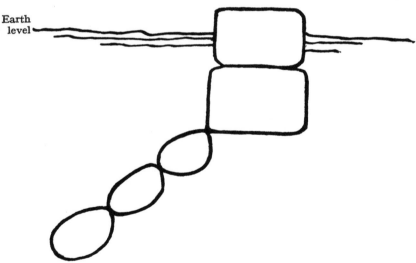

As far as I could ascertain, a part of the foot of the hill seems to have been cut away by the people who built the grave and a piece of made ground added, on the down side, to the small platform thus created, the whole space being just large enough to receive the tomb.

When the foundations of the tomb, if they may so be called, had been exposed, and the earth on the inner side of the wall cleared away, the squared stones and also the undressed boulders were taken up and relaid, being firmly bound together with cement and, in the case of the squared blocks, placed on a concrete foundation. The next step was to deal with the inner and outer walls of the tomb proper, and here some opposition might have been encountered on the part of the local Malays who were working as coolies for me, but a *kěnduri* (feast) before starting work smoothed the way; and the only stipulations made by the local Imam (priest), who was employed as my headman, were that the headstone of the grave should not be moved and that the earth in the central compartment, where presumably Sheikh Ahmad's body lies[1], should be disturbed as little as possible when moving the large blocks of stone at the sides. These large stones, both of the inner and outer wall of the central part of the tomb, were lifted and placed on a concrete foundation six inches in thickness.

The spaces between the inner and outer walls of the central block were filled with earth as, of course, was also the central chamber. Some subsidence of the contents of the latter had caused the inner row of blocks to cant inwards, especially when they were in contact with the heavy uprights (nos. 4, 5, 6 and 7) and the two horizontal blocks between the uprights (nos. 13 and 18). The uprights and the stones between them, too, had followed this subsidence, and had therefore become tilted towards the central compartment of the grave. The inner wall of the central block of the grave is some few inches higher than the outer, and it thus became apparent that the uprights must have stood on the earth between the two walls, impinging slightly on the outer and

---

[1] Any human remains must, long ago, have been destroyed by termites. The whole structure was riddled with their nests at the time of my visit.

lower wall, but not on the inner. They were thus set up perpendicularly in this position on a thick block of cement, which took the place of the earth removed.

It is scarcely needful to say that no cement or plaster of any kind was originally used in the construction of the tomb. In making the restoration, however, I considered it necessary for the preservation of the monument to bind all the stones together, filling the crevices between them, which hitherto had only contained earth, with concrete and covering this with a coating of cement mixed with sand.

During the excavation of the earth between the inner and outer walls of the central block we came upon three interesting objects. One of these was a blue-and-white porcelain, crackled Ming dynasty bowl with floral ornamentation. This was discovered just underneath the laterite block (no. 18) which lies between the two uprights, nos. 7 and 8. It was embedded right-side-up and, besides earth, contained a number of little water-worn quartz pebbles; but whether these were placed there intentionally or not I am not quite certain, as similar stones occurred in the surrounding soil, though not in such numbers as in the earth in the bowl. The piece of porcelain must have been whole; but got broken when the stone above it was shifted. It had evidently been placed in position and was not merely a piece of crockery which had been thrown away. The second object discovered was the greater part, in pieces, of a low and rather pot-bellied Chinese vessel with a wide mouth. This is not of porcelain; but of a fine-grained yellowish clay. It is covered with a thin and flaky ivory-like glaze and has some under-glaze patterns in rather dark blue. These designs are typically Chinese.

The third object was discovered at the head of the tomb between stones nos. 3[1] and 27. This is a curiously carved piece of sandstone some 35 cm. in length. It was placed against the headstone (no. 3) and on the top of a small squared block of laterite. It is difficult to say with certainty

---

[1] The stone marked no. 41 in the plan is a loose block, evidently taken from elsewhere quite recently.

what the carved stone is meant to represent; but I am inclined to think that it is a winged phallus, a most unorthodox object to place in the tomb of a Mohammedan holy man.

The discovery of this peculiar stone much astonished the Malays who were working for me, and they were inclined to treat it with considerable reverence, so much so that when I, after some difficulty, persuaded them to try to move it, and one man had done so without result, owing to its being firmly cemented to the headstone with that peculiar hardened earth which is found in nests of the termite, they announced that it "didn't want to move," and that they dared not make further attempt. Thus I had to do this, to their minds, dangerous piece of work myself. When I had moved the stone, I found that there was a hole in the block of laterite on which it rested: this I probed and found that it extended downwards for about a foot, but what its purpose can have been I do not know. I was prevented from fully excavating and temporarily removing this stone by the superstitious fears of the Malays.

There seem to be some slight traces of mounds and ditches on the land enclosed in the reserve.

In addition to the remains already described, there is a curious grave with a laterite gravestone on a hill on the other side of the road from the Mohammedan tomb and the granite monoliths. The grave is surrounded by an edging of laterite blocks and its orientation is not that of a Mohammedan tomb[1]. Whether it is of the same age as the granite monoliths is problematical, but, as can be seen from the annexed rough sketches, it presents features which are strikingly similar to those of old Javanese gravestones of the Hindu period which are to be seen in the Museum at Batavia[2]. Possibly stones of this type are derived from the leaf of the

---

[1] This grave is, however, regarded as *kĕramat* by the Malays, though offerings are seldom made at it now. It is said that formerly, when Sheikh Ahmad's tomb was covered by jungle undergrowth and difficult to find, this was in great favour as it was easy of access from the river.

[2] The Javanese stones sketched are all in the Museum at Batavia.

Ficus religiosa, the shape of the leaf being very clearly defined in the case of certain backstones of Hindu sculptures from Java[1].

A very small, loose, gravestone of somewhat similar type was found lying on the side of the hill which is directly above Sheikh Ahmad's tomb. I removed this and placed it under cover of the roof over the *kĕramat*.

Before bringing this paper to a close, it may, perhaps, be worth while to try and see if any comparisons can be made between the granite megaliths at Linggi and megalithic monuments occurring in neighbouring countries, or in those whose peoples have blood or other connections with the present or former inhabitants of the Malay Peninsula.

Megalithic monuments are found in Indonesia, as well as in those regions of North-Eastern India which are so intimately connected with Indonesia and also with the Malay Peninsula. Alignments of stones and other megaliths are erected by the Khasis, the Nagas, the Mikirs, the Ho-Mundas and other tribes of North-Eastern India[2]. The Khasis set up stone monuments for the following purposes:

(*a*) As seats for the spirits of the departed.

(*b*) To commemorate a parent or relation.

(*c*) To mark the position of tanks, the water of which is supposed to cleanse the ashes and bones of those who die unnatural deaths.

(*d*) As seats for weary travellers (flat stones).

Groups of stones of class (*b*) consist usually of three, five, seven or nine uprights with flat table-stones in front, the uprights being called male and the recumbent female stones.

In Nias standing stones are set up for the spirits of ancestors to lean against and table-stones are placed for them to use

---

[1] The silver fringes on Malay hangings are still called *daun budi*, because the pendants are more or less in the shape of the leaves of the *Ficus religiosa*, the *bohdi* (Skr.) or peepul tree.

[2] (*a*) *The Khasis*, by P. R. T. Gordon, 1914; (*b*) *The History of Upper Assam*, by L. W. Shakespear, 1914.

as seats, though megaliths are erected for other purposes as well[1]. Some, but by no means all, of the Nias megaliths have a phallic significance[2].

In British North Borneo, according to my own experience, the Dusuns sometimes place rows of stones outside villages, these being thought to act as a protection against disease; and similar guardian stones are also found among the Tinguians of the Philippine Islands[3].

Megalithic monuments occur, too, in many other islands of the Indian Archipelago, and an account of them, in those parts of Indonesia where he thinks that no cultural influences associated with Brahmanism, Buddhism or Islam have penetrated, is to be found in W. F. Perry's *Megalithic Culture of Indonesia.*

This author considers that certain beliefs and customs are intimately connected with the immigrants who introduced the megalithic culture into North-Eastern India and Indonesia. Among these are several which are still found among the Malays or among the wild tribes of the Peninsula, such as a belief that stone implements are thunderbolts[4], prohibitions against eating the flesh of certain animals[5], and ideas that certain actions which are regarded as impious will be punished by disaster of particular kinds happening to the offenders. Stories about such incidents the author calls "punishment tales."

In the Peninsula I know of instances of these "punishment" beliefs among the Malays of Central Pahang, the Negritos of Perak, and the Sakai of South Perak. I tabulate the offences and the punishments which follow them below.

---

[1] *Nias*, by E. E. W. G. Schröder, 1918.

[2] Phalli are carved on them.

[3] There is an illustration of a Tinguian man making an offering to some small guardian stones in *Customs of the World*, vol. II, p. 658.

[4] Generally current among the Malays.

[5] Sakai women and children are prohibited, or will not eat the flesh of certain animals. That of the mousedeer and of the Bĕrok and Kĕra monkeys is commonly regarded as prohibited. The flesh of the white variety of the buffalo is regarded as *pantang* (tabu) by some Malays.

Nationality	Nature of offence	Punishment
Malays	Dressing up and laughing at a cat and dog.	Thunderstorms and village swallowed by earth.
Sakai	(a) Burning jungle leeches in the cook-house fire.	Thunderstorms causing, most probably, the death of the offender.
	(b) Putting *malau* (stick-lac) into the fire. (c) Teasing a monkey, or dressing it up like a man and laughing at its antics. (d) Roasting an egg in the fire. (e) Laughing at snakes or other animals. (f) Imitating the notes of certain birds or the noise made by the cicada.	Among the Sungkai Sakai it is related that the house of an offender against one of these tabus was struck by lightning and swallowed by the earth, hot springs arising on its site. His daughters were killed by a dragon, and this animal and the daughters' leaf dresses—the girls were probably eaten—have become stones. This is the only case of petrifaction for breaking a tabu that I have come across in the Malay States.
Negritos.	(a) Copying the notes of, or killing, certain kinds of birds. (b) Sexual intercourse within the camp.	Thunderstorms, lightning and floods, involving the deaths of the offenders.

There still remains to be discussed the object for which the granite monoliths were erected. It is interesting to note that the Mikirs set up standing stones and place flat slabs in front of them; for the *Pĕdang*, the *Sudu*, and the *Kĕmudi*, each have a slab placed on the ground in this position, while these large uprights are also three in number, as among the Mikirs, or, if we also take into account the two smaller stones (nos. 103 and 104), five, also a Mikir number. Excavation at the main group of monoliths produced no proof that they marked the site of a grave or graves; in fact rather the reverse, for the ground under the table-stones seemed never to have been disturbed previously. I am inclined, therefore, to think that the probabilities are in favour of the Linggi monoliths being either memorial stones (possibly for the use of the spirits of the departed) or guardian stones;—if they should be contemporaneous with the tomb, memorial stones. This, however, would denote a great confusion of beliefs, Mohammedan and pagan.

One other point is perhaps worth mentioning; and that is with regard to the blocks of stone which are placed under the flat slabs in front of the main group of monoliths. These may, of course, be merely for the purpose of preventing the slabs above from sinking into the ground, but it must be remembered that the Khasis build small dolmens, and similar structures are found in Sumba[1]. The following is a description of a small but typical Khasi table-stone: "In front of the line of menhirs is a large flat table-stone resting on stone supports, the top of the uppermost plane being some 2 or 2½ feet from the ground; this flat stone is sometimes as much as a foot or more thick[2]." From this description it looks very much as if the flat stones in front of the Linggi uprights (menhirs) might be rather degenerate relations of the Khasi table-stones. In this connection it is particularly worthy of remark that four undressed boulders of laterite were found under the largest slab, *i.e.* that in front of the *Pĕdang*.

[1] *Vide* illustration in *Megalithic Monuments of Indonesia*, p. 15.
[2] *The Khasis*, p. 146.

PLATE X

THE MOHAMMEDAN TOMB AFTER RESTORATION

PLATE XI

"THE SHIELD OF THE SAINT"
(Pĕrisai: no. 95)

PLATE XII

THE *KEMUDI* OR RUDDER: NO. 94

PLATE XIII

Author's photograph

THE MAIN GROUP OF GRANITE MONOLITHS AT PENGKALAN KEMPAS
AFTER RESTORATION

PLATE XIV

Author's photograph

SMALL GRANITE UPRIGHT AND LATERITE BLOCKS AFTER RESTORATION (NOS. 130–3)

PLATE XV

Small gravestone found at Kĕramat S. Udang on hill above Sheik Ahmad's tomb

Rough sketch of
laterite gravestone from Kĕramat
S. Udang, Linggi, Negri Sembilan

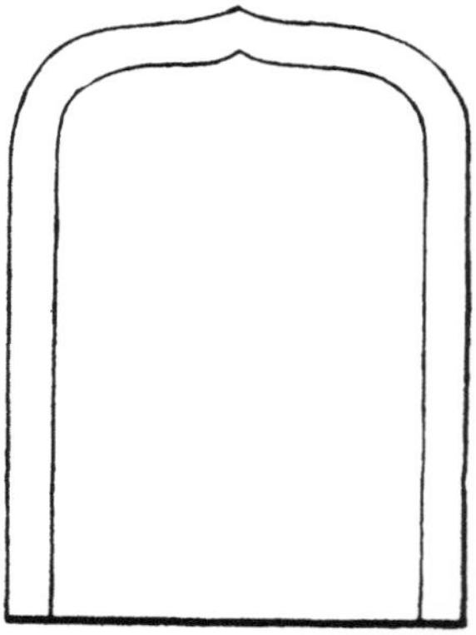

Tombstone of the
Hindu period, Java

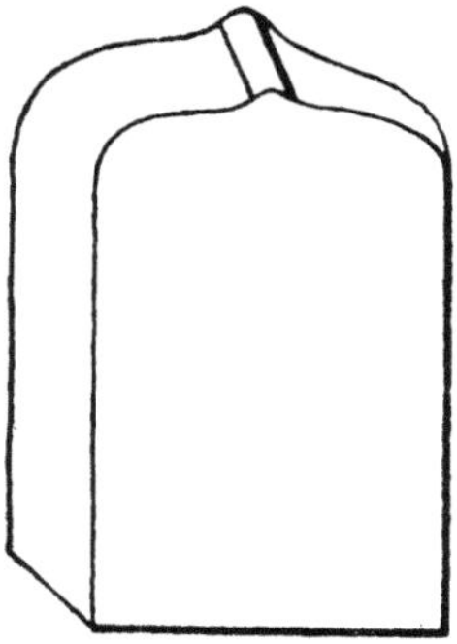

Tombstone of the
Hindu period, Java

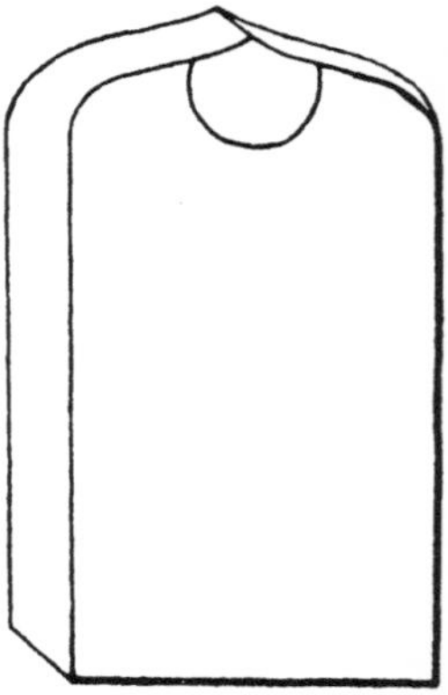

Tombstone of the
Hindu period, Java

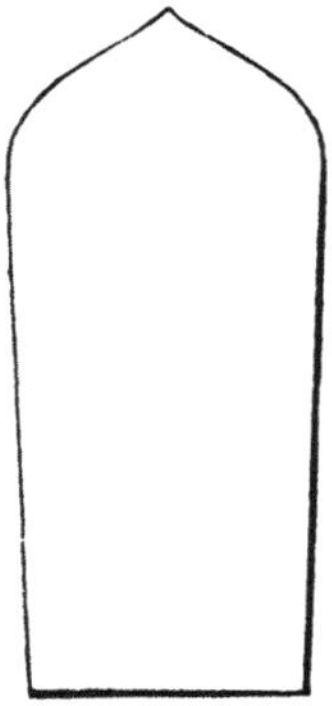

The back of a Statue of the Hindu period. Java

(Sketches not to scale.)

XIX. ON THE ANCIENT STRUCTURES ON KEDAH PEAK

It has been known for a good number of years that ancient remains exist on Kedah Peak. They were first discovered by Mr F. W. Irby, Perak Trigonometrical Survey, in 1894, through his coolies accidentally setting fire to the peaty deposit which then covered the whole of the mountain top. On the fire burning out, a platform about sixteen feet square was disclosed, this being edged with two courses of dressed granite blocks. A hole, with a diameter of about two-and-a-half feet and a depth of two feet, was found in the centre of the platform. The space surrounding this "well" and within the granite-edged square, was, if I understand Messrs Irby's and Lefroy's reports[1] correctly, filled with bricks of roughly dressed laterite.

In addition to the above-mentioned platform (marked A in Mr Irby's plan) he found traces of nine small "hearths" on the southern and precipitous edge of the summit, and those of another platform or "large hearth," with a hole (C) not far from it, at the south-western end of the mountain top. Furthermore, he and Mr Lefroy were able to trace the remains of a rubble wall running from the south-western end of the summit in a north-easterly direction for 160 or 170 feet, finally disappearing under the unburnt remainder of the peat. Roughly north-west of the platform (A), too, another hole was encountered which is marked B on their plan.

On June 16th, 1921, accompanied by Mr W. M. Gordon, Temporary Assistant, F.M.S. Museums, I started excavation work on the mountain.

A preliminary inspection of the summit unfortunately only confirmed what I had heard previously—that the constructors of the present survey beacon had plundered the remains discovered by Mr Irby, using the stones and bricks so obtained in making foundations for the iron legs of the beacon. This

---

[1] *Journal of the F.M.S. Museums*, vol. I, pp. 76–81.

act of vandalism was quite unnecessary, as there is plenty of the local quartz-sandstone to be obtained with a little trouble.

Nearly the whole of the mountain top appearing to be almost bare rock, I decided to deal with the eastern end, the only part which looked at all promising, for it was here only that the peaty deposit remained intact, since it had not been burnt at the time of Mr Irby's visit.

Starting work from the edge of the hole (B)[1] which was found by Mr Irby, the coolies cleared away the peat and earth to a depth of from two to two-and-a-half feet. It then became evident that what had appeared to be a hole with slightly elevated edges, was a depression in the top of a truncated cone which had been constructed of rubbly bricks. The cone was faced with blocks of dressed granite, with bricks interspersed in places, on the side nearest to the platform and hole (A) discovered by Mr Irby. Furthermore this sheathing was continued as a rough pavement to the edge of the remains of Mr Irby's platform. The rest of the cone was without sheathing. Rough measurements of the cone are as follows: depth, after excavation to bedrock, just over one metre; diameter four metres (*circa*). The pavement had a maximum breadth of four metres.

Excavation of the depression at the apex of the cone resulted in the discovery of only one object of interest. This was a ring-stone of granite. It was encountered at a depth of three feet and its material is the same as that of the dressed granite blocks. Its exterior diameter is roughly 23 cm., while that of the hole is 12·5 cm., the breadth of the edge in any one place being roughly 5·5 cm. and the depth about 10 cm.

Some burnt remains, seemingly of former vegetation, were encountered in a little bay on the north-western side of the pavement, close to Mr Irby's platform. These remains extended also under the pavement, as was proved by digging away a little earth. The probability is, therefore, that the

[1] *Vide* plan.

vegetation of the hilltop was burnt off before the pavement
was laid.

Charcoal was fairly common in the soil around the cone
and pavement, but was not present in large quantities. Some
was also met with in the hollow in the cone.

The platform found by Mr Irby, as remarked above, has
been almost totally destroyed, but a rubbly brick foundation, on which it had rested, was laid bare when a small
amount of humus was scraped away, and also a fragment
of the pavement itself—composed of bricks and granite
blocks, not of laterite—as well as three of the granite edging
stones, still in position. Excavation of the hole in the centre
yielded nothing of interest, as a large boulder, possibly
merely an outcrop of the local rock, was encountered almost
immediately, and, as the removal of this, if possible, would
have involved further destruction, I decided not to make an
attempt.

When these parts of the remains had been explored, I
turned my attention to the northern edge of the mountain-
top in the vicinity, for here also the peaty deposit had not
been burnt. On stripping this away we came across rubbly
bricks embedded in earth, forming a rough platform and a
slight glacis on the slope of the hill and, in clearing the loose
rubble, we found three fragments of stone rings, similar to
that described above. The platform abutted on the remains
at A, discovered by Mr Irby, as well as on the pavement and
cone unearthed by myself. The glacis may be the continua-
tion of the rubble wall mentioned by Mr Lefroy. All trace
of this wall in the open now seems to have disappeared. The
remains may have been plundered to form the foundation
for the beacon, but it is more probable that they were
destroyed when the present path to the top of the mountain
was constructed.

With regard to the row of nine so-called fire-places,
mentioned as running along the precipitous southern edge of
the mountain top, very slight traces can now be seen. Mr
Lefroy speaks of finding "indications of nine small hearths,

about four feet square," but I was only able to trace some of these and, even then, the identifications were in most cases doubtful, with the exception of the two near the cone (B), as the soil of the summit had been swept away almost to bedrock.

On exploring the extreme south-western end of the summit, a hole, apparently the same as that shown in Mr Irby's plan (C), was discovered. This appeared to me to be a comparatively recently dug well. Three dressed blocks of granite were found near it on the surface, but these may have been moved to their present position at a recent date. Digging in the hole, which was carried down to bedrock, produced nothing, neither is it lined with brick as are those in the cone and the pavement. Indications of the large hearth, marked on Mr Irby's plan as lying near C, are still to be seen, but nothing of interest was found there.

Little restoration work could be attempted, but the stone and brick sheathing of the cone and the pavement were treated with cement, the cracks between the stone and bricks being filled in with this material, partly in order to preserve the remains against weathering, partly in order to discourage future plunderers. Furthermore, as many of the dressed granite slabs as could be found—either at the base of the beacon, or elsewhere—were collected and placed round the edge of the foundations of the square platform which was discovered by Mr Irby, the rest of the space between this and the hole (A) being filled in with pieces of brick, so as to form a rough reconstruction of the pavement. No cement was used here. Mr Irby has put it on record that the granite edging of the pavement consisted of two courses, but we were not able to collect a sufficient number of stones to carry out the restoration according to his description.

A striking fact about the materials used in the construction of the remains on Kedah Peak is their miscellaneous, and often fragmentary, nature. The granite blocks vary considerably in size and some of them are chamfered at one edge, the edges being sometimes rounded, sometimes angular.

The bricks, too, were of at least three types, and, when found undisturbed, as in the pavement, were merely broken pieces. One or two fragments show signs of glaze, but in the case of some, which have a blackish, shining coating on them, I believe that this is due to the fusion of chemicals, naturally present in the clay, when the bricks were baked. Other pieces have a light greenish crackled glaze on them, but the irregular nature of its distribution here again inclined me to believe that the glazing is accidental, and not intentional. One type of brick, of a light yellow clay, was, when first uncovered, particularly friable, but seemed to harden to a certain extent when exposed to the atmosphere.

As far as I was able to observe, on the sheathed side of the cone and on the pavement, the materials had often been used without any attempt at classification and just as they came to hand—here a brick and there a slab of granite. No kind of mortar or cement was used throughout the construction, and the work was extremely rough. Where granite slabs with chamfered edges were employed—there were a few in the pavement—I could not see that in their disposal any special use had been made of them. I am inclined to think, therefore, that from the indiscriminate use of the materials and their somewhat fragmentary nature they were very likely obtained from some pre-existent building and were transported to the mountain top to be used a second time.

Other points which have still to be dealt with are the purpose of the buildings and their age. It is much to be regretted that our excavations did not throw more light upon these two problems. It is obvious that such a mass of material would not have been transported with so much trouble to the top of a high mountain unless for some reason which was, at any rate, sufficiently cogent to those who were responsible for undertaking the work.

A suggestion has been made by Mr Lefroy that the top of the mountain might possibly have been used as a sort of lighthouse, "signal fires being kept burning to guide mariners, sailing from Sumatra at night," but, as he says immediately after this, "it is improbable materials such as cut granite and bricks would have been carried 4000 feet up a mountain side to form a base for a signal fire when there was any quantity of sandstone, much easier to work, ready to hand."

For myself, I feel certain that the reason for these structures must be sought in religion. In many religions there is a tendency to consider the tops of high mountains as sacred, and sacred mountains are recognised both in Buddhism and Hinduism. Now, though there is a possibility that Mohammedans (Malays after their conversion to Mohammedanism) may have been responsible for the remains on Kedah Peak, yet there is no reason for ascribing them to a date after the advent of Mohammedanism, in fact rather the reverse, since the present Malay inhabitants of the country knew nothing of them until their discovery by Mr Irby, though, when once discovered, they were not backward in inventing stories to account for them.

Now providing that the people who built on Kedah Peak were the same as those who were responsible for the cutting of the granite slabs and the making of the bricks, they must have reached a stage in civilization considerably higher than that of the present-day Malays. The probability is that, judging by other remains which have been found in the country, they were by religion either Hindus or Buddhists, or both, for both Hinduism and Buddhism were, at one time, co-existent and co-operative in Java, and even in India, as they are at the present day in Bali, and to a small extent in Burma and Siam, where, though the people are more Buddhist than anything else, Brahmin priests are still employed in certain state and other ceremonies.

Unfortunately the objects found during excavation throw but little light on the date of the Kedah Peak remains. With the exception of some fragments of Chinese porcelain, all parts of a single plate, no pottery of any kind was encountered, nor were any objects of bronze, iron, or other metal. I am, furthermore, very doubtful whether the pieces of Chinese porcelain, blue-and-white ware, which I ascribe to a late period of the Ming dynasty, are contemporaneous with the stone and brick remains. One fragment of the plate was found directly under the peaty deposit and the others at no great depth, chiefly near Mr Irby's platform (A). The pieces may very possibly have worked down through the peat to the position in which they were found. Plates of the type and period are still in use among Malays in out-of-the-way parts of the country and specimens of this and of older wares are often brought to the towns by hawkers of curiosities, who have purchased them in the Malay Peninsula or Sumatra.

What the remains on Kedah Peak are must still remain problematical, but I think it possible that the conical structure may have been a *dagoba*, the ring-stone, perhaps, crowning its summit. The hole (A) which Mr Irby discovered in the pavement presents a problem which I cannot attempt to solve. It appears to have been too shallow to have made a satisfactory well.

PLATE XVII

Scale $\frac{1}{810}$

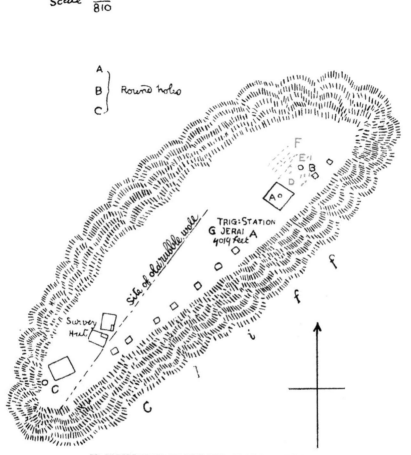

A ⎫
B ⎬ Round holes
C ⎭

F
E
B
D
A °

TRIG: STATION
G JERAI A
4019 feet

Site of durable wall

Survey Hut

O C

C

f

f

i

Mʀ IRBY'S PLAN OF THE TOP OF KEDAH PEAK
WITH NEW DISCOVERIES MARKED IN RED

D Pavement; E Cone; F Glacis

PLATE XVIII

Author's photographs
ANCIENT REMAINS ON KEDAH PEAK

(1) Sheathing of Cone and the Pavement (after treatment with cement)
(2) Attempted Reconstruction of Mr Irby's Platform. The Cone is seen behind

PLATE XIX

GRANITE RING, TWO TYPES OF BRICKS AND CHAMFERED
GRANITE SLAB FROM KEDAH PEAK

XX. ANTIQUITIES FROM SUNGAI BATU ESTATE, SOUTH KEDAH

About the middle of 1921, after finishing some excavation work at the top of Kedah Peak, I went with Mr J. J. Picton Davies, of Sungai Patani, to visit Sungai Batu Estate, since he had informed me that an ancient stone statue and some brickwork had been discovered there. On arriving at the estate, I was shown a mound, consisting largely of laterite, whose measurements were about thirty-nine by fifty-seven feet. Its height was difficult to judge owing to the fact that termites had constructed a big nest on the site. The mound had been, I understood, originally more or less round in outline, but had been partly dug away to obtain laterite for road metal, and a square trench had also been cut round it. At the base of the mound, where it had been intersected by the ditch, three or four courses of stones, rounded by river action, could be observed. They were firmly bedded in hard laterite. A few scattered bricks could be seen in the earth above the stones. They were red and of considerable breadth. I was informed that nothing of interest was found when the mound was prospected for laterite.

The statue, to which I have referred above, was discovered about a hundred yards away, lying loose on the banks of a small river, the Sungai Bujang, which runs through the estate. It is obviously of ancient Hindu origin and probably represents, according to M. Coedés, who has seen a photograph of it, Devi (Durga), the consort of Çiva, triumphing over the Mahishasura, an evil spirit in the form of a buffalo. The figure, which is 67 cm. high, is of a fine-grained granite. It is, unfortunately, much weathered, but, as far as it is possible to judge, the treatment of the subject has been fairly vigorous. A club-like object is borne in the right hand, and, on the left-hand side, where two arms are visible, one is raised and holds a rather crescent-shaped object, while the other hangs beside the body. The feet of the image rest upon a buffalo's head. This statue was kindly presented to the Perak Museum by Mr A. E. G. Darke, Manager of Sungai Batu Estate.

Early in 1923, as I had to pass through Kedah when returning from Kelantan, I again paid a hurried visit to Sungai Batu and was rewarded by obtaining four other interesting stones, which were produced for me by the then Acting Manager.

Three of these are figured in Plate XXI. Two (figs. 1 and 2) look as if they might have formed parts of a conduit for water. One is a rectangular, dressed block of granite with a deep, square channel in it; the other, which is of the same material, appears to be a natural, water-worn boulder which has had a similar channel cut in it, and seemingly has been dressed to a flat surface on that side. These specimens were rescued from the rough stone walling of an estate drain. Of the third stone, depicted on Plate XXI, little can be said with certainty. It is a natural water-worn granite boulder, but certain projections have, I think, been "touched up" to give a semblance of a human form to it.

The fourth stone that I got in 1923 has been so much damaged that I have not had it photographed for illustration. According to the account of a Tamil coolie, who pointed it out to me as it lay in one of the fields of the estate, it had borne a bas-relief of an elephant-headed god (Ganeça). Unfortunately, however, as I was told, the coolies had smashed the figure for road metal. All that now remains is a large block of granite—chiselled to a flat surface at the back and showing the chisel marks very clearly—having a curved oval plaque in front on which the figure formerly stood out in relief. Traces of this are still discernible, and what is presumably the tip of "Ganeça's trunk" remains towards the edge of the plaque, and part of his side in its centre[1].

During my most recent visit to Sungai Batu (1925) I not only collected more carved stones—through the kindly help

---

[1] Dr P. V. van Stein Callenfels, who has recently inspected the stone, believes that it was a *nandi* (Çiva's "vehicle," a bull). I think that he is right and that "Ganeça's trunk" is really the *nandi's* tail.

of Mr Darke and of his assistants Messrs Pearse and Sandars —but carried out some excavations at the mound which I have mentioned above.

It will, perhaps, be as well to deal with these stones first. They had been, or were, found here and there on the surface of the different fields of the estate. One of them (Plate XXII, fig. 2) is a highly conventionalized, ancient, Hindu representation of the female sex organs (*yoni*). The *lingam* (male organ) was not found. The material of the *yoni* appears to be quartzite. It was obtained from Mr Darke, and is said to have been found on field 18. Another (Plate XXII, fig. 1) is a sharpening stone which bears obvious traces of the constant use to which it has been put, and has two cup-like depressions on either side. These were picked out with some pointed tool, the marks of which are still distinct. They were no doubt for holding the water with which the stone was wetted when tools were being sharpened. This object was picked up in field 19, close to the mound which I excavated. The two stones with curious spiral markings (Plate XXII, figs. 3 and 4) were found not far away from each other. The better specimen came from a hill on field 30 *a*, on which Mr Davies formerly had a bungalow, while an assistant on the estate. I also found a squared piece of granite there and some laterite blocks, but nothing else. The worse specimen was discovered on field 37, below the hill. Rumour said that the Raja Bersiong (the tusked raja), about whom so many stories are told, had a palace on the hill. I am not able to state the uses of these two stones, unless they are terminals of balustrades. I think this probable, since I have found a similar stone figured in the *Ceylon Journal of Science* (Section G, vol. I, part II, Plate XIV).

The head of Çiva's bull, the *nandi* (Plate XXIII) was given to me by Mr Darke. He informed me that it came from field 19, that in which the laterite mound, the site of my excavations, is situated.

Let us now consider what some of these specimens indicate. They certainly show that some early inhabitants of Sungai

Batu were Hindus, and worshippers of Çiva or related deities, for we have obtained images of Durga (his consort), (?) Ganeça (son), the *nandi* (his *vahan*, vehicle) on which he rides, and of the *yoni*, always associated with the worship of Çiva or with that of deities of the Çiva group.

After examination, I decided that it might be worth while to excavate the mound that I have mentioned previously. A walling, which was eventually found to consist of laterite blocks, was slightly exposed on the southern side of the mound. This was followed up in both directions along its front, and a mass of termite nest removed from it above. There was then revealed a wall, three feet eight inches high, seven feet two inches long, and two feet eight inches broad, resting upon a foundation of rounded boulders. Its direction was east and west. This wall had a slight but quite distinct plinth both on its outer and inner sides and was canted inwards to some extent. At its western end it disappeared into a mound of laterite, seemingly an original structure, which I did not, therefore, disturb, contenting myself by merely removing overlying termite nests. Towards the east, the wall also disappeared into a laterite mound, and here, as also at its western extremity, a slight walling appeared to spring from its face at right angles.

I next started work on the inner side of the main wall. Here we gradually uncovered what appears to have been a small chamber, which may have had two entrances, one on the north-west, the other on the east. The northern wall of the structure, of which only traces remain, is double. The outer section shows some large flat bricks ("tiles" in the plan) at its end and in its lowest course. The western wall is enclosed in the laterite mound.

The eastern side of the chamber had two remarkable slotted slabs embedded in laterite cement at a low level in the slight remains of its wall. These had bricks arranged along their edges. They had the appearance of forming the sill of a doorway, and it looked as if posts with morticed ends had been originally set up over the slots. It was remarkable, however, that these slots, when discovered, had small, squared stones covering them. The large granite *yoni* figure in Plate XXVI (fig. 2) was discovered almost immediately above these slabs[1]. It was resting, upside-down, with its "spout" directed towards the southern wall. It seems possible that entrance to this doorway, if such it was, was obtained past the visible end of the wall, eastwards, where there appeared to be a passage through the mound.

In the plan which is reproduced with this paper, for which I have to thank Captain P. M. Leckie of the Kedah Survey Department, it will be noticed that, in certain places, ends of walls are marked as "lost in rubbish" or as ending in "rubbish." This so-called rubbish appears to me to be laterite which has purposely been placed in the position in which it is now, having been used as a cement. I may be wrong about this, but I did not consider it wise to clear it away, possibly thus destroying some of the original structure on the chance of finding the walls continued underneath.

The bedding of boulders in a cement of laterite has already been mentioned. This substance is soft when first dug, but hardens on exposure. This method of construction is clearly to be seen at the base of the mound on the west of the shrine.

The eastern mound is indefinite in shape and outline. It has an extension in, or on, which are numbers of boulders and a few bricks. Many of these had been carried up in the termites' nest which formerly crowned it. I had them gathered together when the nest was removed, and subsequently replaced on the mound.

It is curious to note that, during the excavation of the shrine, not one single piece of pottery was found; nor were implements or coins discovered. Fragments of pottery were, however, common on the surface of the soil about one hundred yards away, on either side of the path which passes the mound and leads to the estate factory. Many of these appear to be ancient. Those collected include a fragment of

---

[1] The square hole in the *yoni* is, no doubt, for the insertion of the base of the *lingam*.

a spouted water-bottle (*kendi*) in coarse and thick pottery and some pieces of céladon. Probably there were houses in the neighbourhood, but I am not prepared to say definitely that they were of the same period as the shrine, though it appears likely.

Pieces of a red jar of early type, having originally had four small handles, were obtained from a spot about two hundred yards from the shrine. This jar had been smashed by coolies while weeding, and Mr Darke pointed out the spot where the remains were lying. It has been found possible to reconstruct the vessel and an illustration of it accompanies this paper (Plate XXVII).

It would seem not unlikely that the Hindu inhabitants of Sungai Batu, who built the shrine, were foreign traders or miners in early times, not Malays. If they were Malays, they certainly learnt the art of stone-carving from Indian sources. Sungai Batu Estate extends to a large navigable river, the Merbok, up which traders might be expected to make their way. The Sungai Bujang would provide settlers with a constant supply of beautifully clear water. I have remarked that this stream is not far distant from the shrine. This stands on fairly high ground, and inspection of the little river valley inclines me to the opinion that the stream has shifted its course, and once ran even closer to it than it does to-day.

A point which may be further emphasized is the mixture of materials which were used in constructing the shrine—laterite blocks, laterite concrete, river boulders, bricks and dressed stones. Their miscellaneous nature, and often haphazard use, is reminiscent of the manner in which the ancient structures on Kedah Peak—at no great distance—were built. One brick from the shrine had a chamfered edge, while two others were tongued.

In the case of the *nandi* it seems possible that the figure was purposely destroyed by Mohammedans (? Malays after their conversion to Islam). We have only a portion of the head: the muzzle and the whole of the body are missing.

The breakages appear old, and a granite statue is not to be destroyed unless considerable force is used. The shrine, too, may, from its dilapidated condition, also have undergone rough treatment of a similar nature.

Traces of another mound, smaller than that which I excavated, exist close to the Sungai Bujang and near the factory. The material of it was, I believe, removed for use as road metal and all that now remains is a circular pit, slightly raised at the edges, in the sides of which a few bricks can be seen arranged one above the other. It is said that considerable quantities of bricks were obtained in digging, but nothing else.

Undoubtedly Sungai Batu has a long history, extending from the time when stone implements were in use—for a beautifully made axe-head of chalcedony was purchased from a Tamil coolie who had found it—through the Hindu period. Remains referable to ancient Mohammedan occupation are also to be seen, and a group of four graves, evidently, from the shape and elaborate nature of the stones on them, those of Mohammedans and of royalty or important persons, are to be found towards the Merbok River in field 79. These graves constitute what is known as the Makam Langgar. The Malays did not seem to know whose bodies were buried there, though one suggested the Raja Bersiong, and another spoke of a raja of Setul. Two of the graves are those of males, two of females, as is denoted by the styles of the stones. Each grave bears a pair of these. They are without inscriptions, and their material appears to be a sandstone of some kind, probably of the variety often called *batu Acheh*. The female stones are of the flattened "Chinese lantern" type, their outline being probably taken from a lotus bud viewed from the side. They are similar, but one pair is larger than the other. The male stones are peg-shaped, and one pair is larger than the other. The smaller couple (one of which is illustrated) have unusual lotus-bud tops and a curious type of decoration on their stems. The larger pair are of somewhat similar type, but the ornamentation is less pronounced. A photograph of the best of the two was attempted but, owing to bad lighting, was not very successful. The Malays consider the graves, from the variation in the sizes of the stones, to be those of a raja and his wife and of their son and daughter. Though they are obviously those of Mohammedans, strong Hindu influence is to be detected in the lotus *motif* of the tombstones.

While I was working on Sungai Batu, Mr Darke informed me that a small canister, about the size of the round tins which contain fifty cigarettes, and full of ancient Malay gold coins, had been discovered about five years previously by Tamil women who were employed as weeders. Unluckily none of the Europeans heard of the matter until a fortnight afterwards, and, in the meantime, somebody had said that the coins, being "dead man's money" were unlucky, with the result that they had nearly all been thrown away. Only the less superstitious coolies had preserved a few, and some of these had returned to India. By offering high prices for any that were brought to me, I was able to obtain two good specimens from Tamil women, while Mr Darke kindly gave me another, obtained from his coolies, which had been damaged by the addition of a silver shank. Luckily it will probably be possible to remove this accretion, leaving the coin almost in its original condition, while, even now, it does not hamper identification of the specimen. The two coins that I purchased from the coolies are similar. They bear on the obverse the word "Sultan," in Arabic characters, and on the reverse, (?) "Mua'zam Shah." The third is of a type figured and described by Bucknill in the *Journal of the Royal Asiatic Society, Malayan Branch* (1923, vol. I, pp. 202–204). It bears on one face the inscription *Malik-al-adil*; on the other a figure of some kind of four-legged animal. Millies ascribes coins with a similar inscription to Trengganu, on the strength of a statement by Abdullah bin Abdul Kadir, but I know, from personal experience, that many specimens of the tin "hat-money" of Pahang have a similar legend.

Other Ancient remains near Sungai Batu Estate

Where ancient remains are known to occur in the Kuala Merbok neighbourhood, the Malays unhesitatingly ascribe them to the Raja Bersiong. In the neighbourhood of Sungai Batu Estate, but outside its boundaries, are pointed out what are thought to have been his elephant trap (*pěndiyat*) and the site of one of his houses. His well is stated to be situated somewhere along the coast between Pulau Saiyak and the mouth of the Merbok, while some traces of ancient brick-work are said to be visible at the top of Bukit Meriam, Kuala Merbok—opposite Tanjong Dawai. It may be noted that all this region, and especially Sungai Batu Estate, lies at the foot of Gunong Jěrai (Kedah Peak). Now the old capital of Kedah, Langkasuka, is described in the *Hikayat Marong Mahawangsa* (a Malay history of Kedah, containing much material of a legendary nature) as occupying just such a position[1]. It seems quite possible, therefore, that its site has now been discovered on, and in the neighbourhood of, Sungai Batu Estate.

I visited Bukit Pendiyat, where the elephant trap proved to be a wide and deep oval ditch, enclosing a considerable space, and with an "entry" to, and an "exit" from, the enclosure, places where the ditch had purposely been left incomplete. It seems likely that the Malays are right in their supposition as to the former use of the ditch, and stockades probably converged on its entrance when it was in use. I do not think that it can have been part of a fort, as Malay forts, I believe, were always rectangular, while modern elephant traps are often oval, as in this case. The "house site" on Bukit Pendiyat was also explored. This was towards the other end of the ridge. Nothing was found there with the exception of a slight mound containing some bricks, through which I drove a small trench, and a small brick-lined hollow on the up-hill side of the mound.

[1] Blagden, in the *Journal of the Royal Asiatic Soc., Straits Branch*, no. 53 (1909), pp. 148–149. I have to thank the Hon. Dr R. O. Winstedt for drawing my attention to this portion of Blagden's paper.

PLATE XX

HINDU FIGURE FROM SUNGAI BATU ESTATE, KEDAH

PLATE XXI

One foot.

1   2   3

WORKED STONES FROM SUNGAI BATU ESTATE, SOUTH KEDAH

PLATE XXII

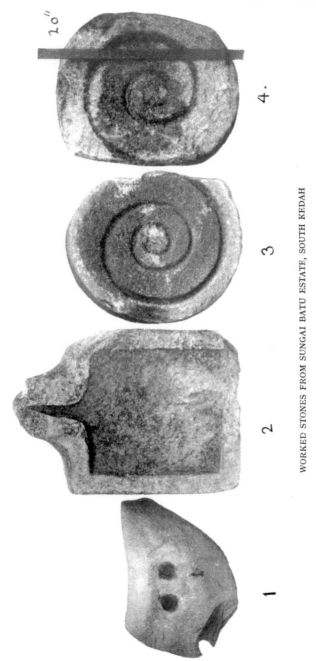

WORKED STONES FROM SUNGAI BATU ESTATE, SOUTH KEDAH

PLATE XXIII

BROKEN HEAD OF *NANDI*, SUNGAI BATU ESTATE, SOUTH KEDAH

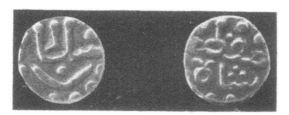

GOLD COIN FROM SUNGAI BATU ESTATE
(Magnification about three diameters)

PLATE XXIV

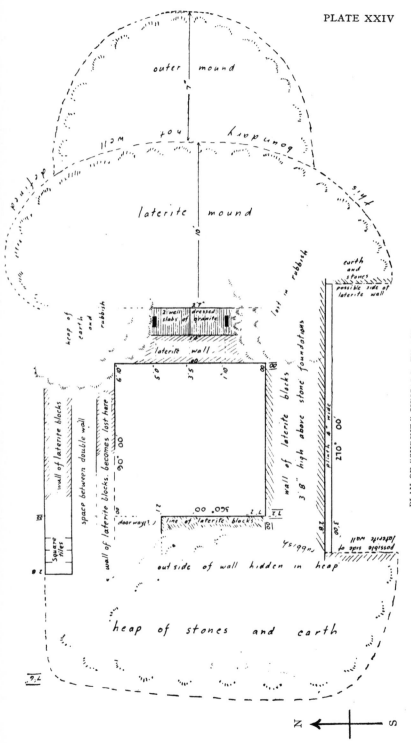

PLAN OF "SHRINE," SUNGAI BATU ESTATE, SOUTH KEDAH

PLATE XXV

Author's photograph

INNER SIDE OF SOUTHERN WALL OF "SHRINE,"
SUNGAI BATU ESTATE

Author's photograph

SOUTHERN WALL OF "SHRINE,"
SUNGAI BATU ESTATE

PLATE XXVI

YONI FOUND IN "SHRINE," SUNGAI BATU ESTATE

"SILL STONES" OF SHRINE, SUNGAI BATU ESTATE

PLATE XXVII

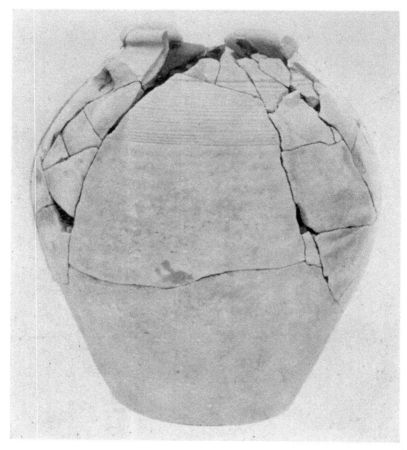

RED EARTHERN JAR, SUNGAI BATU ESTATE

PLATE XXVIII

Author's photograph

MOHAMMEDAN GRAVESTONE (FEMALE),
SUNGAI BATU ESTATE

Author's photograph

MOHAMMEDAN GRAVESTONE (MALE),
SUNGAI BATU ESTATE

XXI. AN ANCIENT CLAY VESSEL FROM THE LANGKAWI ISLANDS

A very valuable addition has recently been made to the collections of the Perak Museum by the acquisition of an ancient clay vessel from one of the Langkawi Islands. The F.M.S. Museums are deeply indebted to the Kedah Government for presenting the specimen; to Tuan Haji Wan Yahya, Secretary to Government, Kedah, and to Major G. M. Kidd for their kind offices in obtaining and forwarding it. The jar was found on Pulau Tuba by Inche Wan Mahmud, District Officer, Langkawi, in a cave which is situated near the path that leads to the summit of Bukit Tuba. Major Kidd has kindly sent me the following description of the cave, given to him by Tungku Kassim, who has paid the place a visit:

On the way up from the seashore to the top of Bukit Tuba, near the track, and not far from the top, was a narrow aperture that one had to crawl through to enter a cave about 20′–30′ across and of a sufficient height to stand up in comfortably. There was an earth floor and the sides of the cave were of white marble, much worn.

There was nothing of special interest to be seen in the cave when it was visited by Tungku Kassim, but the District Officer told him that there had been the broken pieces of another pot in the cave when he took away our specimen.

The vessel is of brownish clay, containing many impurities, such as small stones, and, as compared with the size of the pot, the shard may be considered thin. The bottom is rounded and the body narrowly oviform. The neck and mouth are broad in proportion. The general impression obtained on inspecting the jar is that it is very ancient, and this is heightened by the fact that the body of it is apparently decorated with cord-marking. The pattern seems to have been made by applying a fairly fine cord repeatedly to the wet clay, so that the lines thus produced lie close together and sometimes cross. Fragments of cord-marked pottery frequently occur in the cave deposits of the Peninsula[1].

[1] *Vide* paper XXIV *infra*.

PLATE XXIX

ANCIENT CLAY VESSEL
From Pulau Tuba, Langkawi Islands, Kedah
Measurements: Length 56 cm.; greatest breadth 25·3 cm.

XXII. ON THE PERSISTENCE OF AN OLD TYPE OF WATER-VESSEL

Spouted clay water-vessels are found in the Peninsula at the present day in Negri Sembilan, and the Perak Museum possesses modern locally made examples from Kuala Pilah. There is also in the Museum a single representative of this type of vessel from Kuala Tembeling in Pahang, but the spout is somewhat different from those from Negri Sembilan, and the top much more widely open. The Negri Sembilan specimens are pot-bellied vessels with a spout projecting from the top of the body; they have a rather small aperture at the top, and a slight rim, or foot, below.

In the Museum of the "Bataviaasch Genootschap van Kunsten en Wetenschappen" are some very similar vessels, both ancient and modern, and these are particularly interesting for purposes of comparison with spouted water-pots from the Malay States, as they show that an ancient type of vessel has persisted till the present day[1].

The modern material in the Batavian Museum comes from the west coast of Sumatra and from Acheh. Examples from the former region are most like our Negri Sembilan specimens in that they are open at the top and of rather similar build, though they have not the small rim, or foot, at the bottom; being simply rounded. Those from Acheh are taller, due in part to their being raised on a considerable foot. Their tops are not open, but there is a small round hole in each at the side of the top. They are presumably filled through the spout by submerging the vessels bodily, the small hole being rather to provide an egress for the air, than an entrance for the water. The spouts, too, are longer actually, and in proportion, than those of the pots from Acheh and Negri Sembilan.

[1] My grateful thanks are due to the Committee of the Batavian Society and to Mr Hoedt, formerly Curator of the Ethnographical Section of the Museum, for permission to take the photographs used in this article, and for other help.

Let us now turn to the ancient specimens. Some of these are of Chinese make. One, an old blue-and-white vessel of the Ming dynasty period, has an open top, a rather long straight neck, a short and fat spout, and a slight foot, comparable to that of the Negri Sembilan type. Another, an earthen vessel covered with green glaze, has an open top and a swollen and fluted spout, while the body is ornamented with perpendicular ribbings. A third vessel from the same locality as that last described—they both come from the Salayer Islands—is of fine red clay. It has an open top with a small lid, and a tumid spout. I do not know if it is of Chinese manufacture or not.

Spouted water-vessels are also depicted in Javanese carvings of the Hindu period. One representation of such an utensil is to be seen in the hand of a figure of Bhrkuti, which is in the Batavian Museum. The type here seen has a foot and a closed top, and much resembles the examples from Acheh, the chief difference being that the spout is turned up against the body of the vessel, and ends in an animal's head, the open jaws forming the aperture of the spout.

In addition to this representation, there is also in the Museum a large model of a water-pot in stone. This comes from the Kedoe Residency, and is of the Hindu period. In the Museum *Guide to the Archaeological Collections* (no. 368) it is called a *gĕndi* (*i.e.* Malay *kĕndi*). It has a closed top, and a very short, rather widely open, spout.

The antiquity of this type of water-vessel seems sufficiently well established, and it would appear that we must, probably, look to India as its country of origin, but there is some difficulty in accounting for the specimens from China. I will, however, attempt to deal with this in a little while.

In trying to find prototypes of the Javanese pottery I came across some pictures of vessels from Nĕpal[1] which seem to be nearly related to those from Acheh. They are of metal—probably copper or brass—though their exact

[1] *Journal of Indian Art and Industry*, vol. VI, Plate 29, figs. 1 and 2.

material is not stated. They have fairly large feet, roughly spherical bodies, long necks, open tops, and long spouts which point upwards. One specimen has a head of the well-known fabulous Makara, I believe, at the base of the spout[1].

I think that there cannot be much doubt that this spouted type of vessel found its way from India to Java, but as I have already remarked the question of Chinese vessels of the same description presents more difficulty. Of course it is perfectly possible, indeed likely, that a water-vessel of a style which may well have been used in ceremonies connected with religious purification, found its way from India to China through the agency of Buddhist missionaries and pilgrims, and became established there[2]. I doubt, however, whether spouted water-vessels at all corresponding to those described here are commonly found in China, and it must be remembered that the Chinese, for the promotion of their export trade, especially in later times, frequently copied objects from other countries or produced articles of non-Chinese type which they thought, from their shape, or the nature of their decorations, would find a ready sale among the peoples with whom they traded. In this category comes the so-called Siam-ware, and also certain plates and saucers with Arabic inscriptions—for sale among the Mohammedans of the East Indies—and the "Sino-Persian" ware of the Ming dynasty.

A search through Gulland's two volumes on porcelain has resulted in my finding an illustration of only one spouted vessel which at all resembles the types from the East Indies[3]. The neck of this is long and open at the top, the spout long and shaped like that of a tea-pot, the body hexagonal and having a small foot. It is described as a six-sided wine or spirit decanter.

[1] Cf. the Javanese Hindu-period vessel in the hand of a statue, mentioned above.

[2] Dr Bosch, Director of the Antiquarian Survey of the Dutch East Indies, to whom I spoke about this old form of water-vessel, called it a *kĕndi*, saying that it was a common type in Buddhist countries.

[3] *Chinese Porcelain*, p. 173 and fig. 294.

PLATE XXX

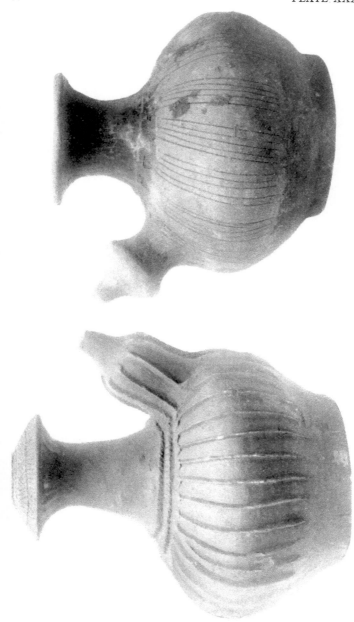

SPOUTED WATER-VESSELS FROM KUALA PILAH, NEGRI SEMBILAN

(Perak Museum, Taiping)

PLATE XXXI

WATER-VESSELS FROM THE WEST COAST OF SUMATRA
(Batavian Society's Museum)

WATER-POTS FROM ACHEH
(Batavian Society's Museum)

PLATE XXXII

MING PERIOD CHINESE VESSEL FROM THE DUTCH EAST INDIES

(Batavian Society's Museum)

PLATE XXXIII

KENDI (GENDI) IN HAND OF A FIGURE OF BHRKUTI
(Tjandi Toempang, afd: Malang, res: Pasoeroean)

(Batavian Society's Museum)

XXIII. NEOLITHIC STONE IMPLEMENTS

Bibliography for papers XXIII–XXVI

1885. HALE, ABRAHAM. "Stone Axes, Perak." *Nature*, vol. XXXII, p. 626.

1888. HALE, ABRAHAM. "Notes on Stone Implements from Perak." *Journal of the Anthropological Institute of Great Britain and Ireland*, vol. XVII, p. 66.

1885. MORGAN, J. DE. "L'âge de la pierre polie dans la presqu'île Malaise." *L'Homme*, Tome II, p. 494.

1891. RIDLEY, HENRY N. "Discovery of a Stone Implement in Singapore." *Journal of the Royal Asiatic Society, Straits Branch*, no. 23, p. 141.

1904. SWAN, R. M. W. "Note on Stone Implements from Pahang." *Man*, no. 34 (April).

1897. WRAY, LEONARD, Jun. "The Cave-Dwellers of Perak." *Journal of the Anthropological Institute of Great Britain and Ireland*, vol. XXVI, no. 1, p. 36. Repr. *Perak Museum Notes*, no. II, part 1. See also *Journ. F.M.S. Museums*, vol. I, pp. 13–15, "Further Notes on the Cave-dwellers of Perak."

1905. MARTIN, Dr RUDOLF. *Die Inlandstämmer der Malayischen Halbinsel*, p. 75.

1906. SKEAT, W. W. and BLAGDEN, C. O. *Pagan Races of the Malay Peninsula*, vol. I, p. 242 et seqq.

1906. SCRIVENOR, J. B. "Notes on the Petrology of Stone Implements from the Federated Malay States." *Journal of the F.M.S. Museums*, vol. I, p. 123.

1918. EVANS, I. H. N. "Preliminary Report on Cave Exploration near Lenggong, Upper Perak." *Journal of the F.M.S. Museums*, vol. VIII, part IV, pp. 227–234.

1920. EVANS, I. H. N. "Preliminary Report on the Exploration of a Rock-shelter in the Batu Kurau Parish of Perak." *Journal of the F.M.S. Museums*, vol. IX, part I, pp. 34–36.

1920. EVANS, I. H. N. "Cave dwellings in Pahang." *Journal of the F.M.S. Museums*, vol. IX, part I, pp. 37–52.

1922. EVANS, I. H. N. "On a Find of Stone Implements at Tanjong Malim." *Journal of the F.M.S. Museums*, vol. IX, part IV, pp. 257–258.

1922. EVANS, I. H. N. "A Rock-Shelter at Gunong Pondok." *Journal of the F.M.S. Museums*, vol. IX, part IV, pp. 267–270.

1925. EVANS, I. H. N. "Stone Implements from Chong, South Siam." *Journal of the F.M.S. Museums*, vol. XII, part II, pp. 54–55.

1925. EVANS, I. H. N. "A Hoard of Stone Implements from Batu Gajah." *Journal of the F.M.S. Museums*, vol. XII, part II, p. 67.

The subject of the occurrence of stone implements in the Malay Peninsula is not one which has yet been fully dealt with, although a fair number of papers and articles with regard to it have appeared at various times. The present notes have been got together in an attempt to embody what has already been published and to add some fresh information to it. All the stone implements which have yet been found in the Peninsula (except some from the Kuantan District of Pahang and the majority of those from cave deposits) appear to be of a true neolithic culture, and it seems that they probably are of much more recent date than those of that type which are found in Europe. The great majority of them are axe or adze heads, and no knives, spear heads or arrow heads of stone have yet been discovered, this being probably due to the fact that hardwoods and bamboo are abundant in the country, the former having most likely been used to some extent for making spear and arrow heads, and the latter for knives and spear heads[1]. It is worthy of note that bamboo spear points are still used by both Malays and aborigines (especially in spear traps for game), and bamboo knives for ceremonial purposes, such as the severing of the navel cord. Another important factor which probably contributed to the neglect of stone as a material for making pointed or sharp-edged implements produced by chipping, is the rarity in the Peninsula of rocks suitable for the purpose, there being no common stone which will give such sharp-edged flakes as flint, nor which will chip so readily and smoothly.

Before proceeding to discuss the question of who were

---

[1] Cf. New Guinea and many of the islands of the Pacific, where stone axes are, or were, recently in use, but not stone spear heads or arrow heads. In the Admiralty Group, where obsidian, an easily chipped material, occurs, spear heads of this material are found.

the makers of these implements, or to describe the types of those that have been found, I propose to give some account of native ideas with regard to them, and some details about situations and localities in which they occur.

To the Malays of the Peninsula stone implements are known as *batu lintar*, *halintar*, or *batu petir*, all three terms meaning thunderbolts. In the Tempassuk District of British North Borneo, they are generally called thunder teeth (*gigiguntor*) from the idea that they are teeth shed, in the form of thunderbolts, by the spirit of thunder. Similar ideas are found in other islands of the Malay Archipelago, were not unknown among the Greeks, and still survive in parts of Europe.

In British North Borneo stone implements are regarded as powerful charms. The spurs (natural) of fighting cocks are rubbed with them in order to ensure their gaining the victory by making deep wounds on the birds opposed to them, and water in which a stone implement has been placed is given to smallpox patients to drink as a remedy, or is sprinkled over the young rice to protect it against misfortunes and to gain a plenteous harvest. So highly are these talismans regarded, that a man is frequently unwilling to show an example in his possession lest its potency should be diminished by it being handled and examined[1]. Similar ideas seem to have been, or are, current in the Malay States, but are, I fancy, rapidly becoming obsolete. Near Kuala Tembeling in Pahang, I found that the Malays were ready to part with stone implements for prices far below those that I had to give in Borneo, nor was I told any of those wonderful tales with regard to their being found at the foot of a coconut tree which had been struck by lightning, such as those with which the Borneo peasants regaled me. The Pahang Malays admitted, fairly enough, that they had come across their specimens in the rice fields, while my Borneo friends did the same if the stones had been discovered by themselves, but produced a fairy story if they had descended to them from their fathers, their grandfathers, or other ancestors.

[1] Paper by the author in *Man*, No. 86, 1913.

The vast majority of the neolithic type stone implements from the Malay Peninsula which are now in museums or private collections have been obtained either from Malay cultivators or Chinese miners. The Malay peasant finds stone implements lying about on the surface of the soil while working in his rice fields. In a draft letter from Mr L. Wray, at that time Curator of the Perak Museum, which is filed among other documents in the office, he says that most of the stone implements in the Museum were found in the *padi* fields. He adds "I have two or three from the mines, and some from river-beds, one found in a tree[1], two picked up on the roads, and one I found in a cave." This information does not throw very much light on the subject of the age of the implements. Specimens from tin mines may have come from the surface soil, and, unless it can be definitely shown that they did not, the same thing also holds good with regard to river beds.

We have, seemingly, instances of stone implements having been found at a great depth, and even ancient wooden objects have been discovered with a thick deposit of alluvial matter covering them. It must be remembered, however, that erosion is rapid in the Malay States. Swan, in an article on stone implements from Pahang (see bibliographical note above), referring to an implement which he does not figure, says, "the rudest implement was found by myself at the bottom of an alluvial gold mine in the Tui Valley in Pahang, and it had not been disturbed in its position when I found it. It lay in a deposit of gravel on crystalline limestone rock, and over it had a deposit of gravel and clay 43 feet thick." Some examples from Batu Gajah, too, are said to have been found at a depth of fifty feet. These formed a hoard.

To turn now to the methods which have been employed in the manufacture of stone implements in the Peninsula. From a survey of the specimens in the Perak Museum, it is quite clear that both chipping and rubbing down have been employed, but, in unfinished specimens, of which we possess

---

[1] A "fairy story," like those told by my Borneo friends?

a fair number, it can be seen that in some cases both processes were made use of, in others rubbing down only was resorted to[1]. With regard to the majority of the finished implements it is not easy to say definitely whether chipping has been employed in their manufacture or not, since they have been so finely ground that all traces of this process would have disappeared. It seems probable, however, that this was the case, since, among the unfinished specimens, the chipped implements are in a majority.

In a large number of apparently unfinished specimens, which do not show chipping, it is a matter of some difficulty to know whether this process was first employed or not, owing to the implements obviously having been much weathered or water-worn subsequent to their manufacture, so as to obliterate traces of either process. They preserve their forms, but the original surface has been lost. I am, however, able to pick out a few, about which I think that there can be little doubt that no chipping process has been employed.

To turn again to the chipped implements, it is remarkable that the work should be so fine considering that the material appears to be generally by no means very amenable to treatment of this kind. Mr J. B. Scrivenor, who has made a microscopical examination of the petrology of seven stone implements from the Tembeling Valley in Pahang, and from Rembau in Negri Sembilan, states that three are made from fine-grained silicious rocks with schistose structure, one from a fine-grained silicious rock without schistosity, two from metamorphosed fine-grained silicious sediment, and one from a fine-grained silicious rock containing angular fragments of quartz. Probably, the rocks from which these seven specimens are made may be taken as being fairly representative of the materials which were employed for making stone implements, though other kinds of rock have some-

[1] These may belong to an older, "middle neolithic," culture. They are generally, if not always, without sides, and have, therefore, a more or less oval section. Specimens polished to a cutting edge only may be classified as "lower neoliths" (protoneoliths).

times been put to this use, notably a kind of yellowish (?) chert and rhyolite.

With regard to the distribution of stone implements in the Malay Peninsula it would seem that in some districts they are by no means uncommon. In the Perak Museum, we have a large collection, and the following States are represented: Kelantan (many specimens), Perak (many specimens, chiefly from Upper Perak and the Larut, Kuala Kangsar and Kinta Districts), Pahang, Kedah and Negri Sembilan. The Selangor Museum possesses examples from Selangor, Negri Sembilan and Pahang, while the Singapore Museum has stone implements from States already mentioned and a single specimen from Singapore Island[1]. In those parts of the Peninsula from which no stone implements have been recorded it is probable that they exist, but that no collections have yet been made. Around Kuala Tembeling, in Pahang, stone implements appear to be extremely common, for while I was in this district, in 1913, I stopped at two or three villages on the Tembeling River on my way upstream, and offered to buy any that the inhabitants might possess. I obtained thirteen specimens in a very short time, and refused several others which were worn or broken and of common types. Mr L. Wray, in the correspondence from which I have quoted above, states that stone implements are rare in Perak and says, "I have not been able to get one in the last two years." Against this, however, is the large number from that State that we have in the Museum collection. A Kuala Kangsar Malay, whom I have questioned recently, tells me that they are by no means uncommon in his district. It may, perhaps, be noted here that stone implements, especially those of a dark colour purchased from Malays, are frequently found to have yellow metallic markings upon them, these being due to their having been used as touch-stones; sometimes also they have their faces and angles worn away by having been employed as hones for sharpening small knives.

[1] Seemingly a "lower neolith."

It may be stated that there are only four types of stone implements, which are common in the Malay States. Specimens of these are figured on Plate XXXIV. Of type 1 the F.M.S. Museums possess specimens from Perak, Pahang, Negri Sembilan and Kelantan, of type 2 from Perak, Pahang, Selangor, Negri Sembilan and Kelantan, of type 3 from Perak, Selangor, Negri Sembilan and Pahang, and of type 4 from Perak and Kelantan.

There are of course some modifications of type. Some specimens of type 3, generally those from Pahang, are very long, others shorter and broader, while those of type 2 may, or may not, be hollow ground on the under surface at the point, and in a few cases the angles of the beak are rounded off, and one implement from Pulau Tiga, Lower Perak, has a central ridge down the back, sloping sides and rounded beak, like Javanese examples. Specimens approximating to type 4—this type is sometimes, but not always, ground equally on both sides—may either have their sides parallel or they may diverge towards the cutting edge, so that the implement is somewhat fan-shaped. In the case of type 1, the variation is generally in the breadth of the cutting edge and the size of the implement, some specimens being very small. Occasionally this type has sides which are sloped inwards towards the surface which is ground away at the cutting edge. From the uneven grinding at the edges of most of our implements, it would appear that they were hafted as adzes rather than axes.

To proceed now to the description of the rarer types, of which, in most cases, the F.M.S. Museums only possess a few examples. In Taiping we have a very remarkable shouldered implement (Plate XXXVI, fig. 2), which very much resembles the modern Malay iron adze head. The tang of this is unfortunately broken off, but enough of it remains to make a reconstruction fairly easy. This form of implement is well known from N.E. India (Mundas), Burma, Siam and Indo-China. Unfortunately, although there does not seem much reason for doubting that the specimen was obtained in the

Peninsula, I have not been able to find any details with regard to the locality in which it was collected. For some reason the records with regard to a large number of the stone implements, obtained before the time of the present departmental staff, are very scanty. Many specimens, from the pencilled inscriptions on them, were obtained from the late Mr A. Hale, formerly an officer in the service of the Government, others including a large number from Kelantan, are simply marked with the name of the State in which they were found.

Another implement of a curious type is a stone which has been used for two purposes. It is an axe head which has a depression on either side. On examination of these, it seems likely that they were made either for, or by, grinding down small stone implements. In the Perak Museum are painted casts of two stone implements of uncommon type which were found in the wash-boxes at the Kenaboi Hydraulic Mine, Jelebu, Negri Sembilan. Two of the casts are figured on Plate XXXVII, figs. 3 and 4. It will be seen that they are quoit-shaped objects, one of them being penannular. The originals are made of a bluish-coloured stone of rather light weight. Other objects, including bronze celts—to which I shall have occasion to refer later—a small piece of smelted bronze, a crucible, tin rings and chains, and an ear-stud of the same material have also come from the Kenaboi wash-boxes, but we have not sufficient data to be able to judge as to whether they are contemporaneous with, or newer than, the stone implements. A painted cast of another quoit-shaped implement, made from a dark brown stone, is also preserved in the Perak Museum, but I have not been able to find out whence it was obtained.

In *Man* (no. 34, 1904) Swan has described certain stone implements found in Pahang, among them being two portions of a quoit-shaped implement, which is evidently of similar type to those from the Kenaboi Mine, this, he states, was found, at a depth of about a foot, in the surface soil near the Tui River. He remarks with regard to these fragments that "they are similar to, but are better formed than, some other rings which were found near the Tenom River at a place fifteen miles further north. One of these is, I believe, in Lancing College at Brighton, and several are in the Museum at Taiping in Perak. The use of the rings is also a mystery. They cannot have been worn on the person as ornaments, and they are too light and fragile to have been used as cutting tools. The only supposition that suggests itself is that they may have been religious symbols." Now the only quoit-shaped implements—obtained previous to the date of his paper—that we have in the Federated Malay States Museums, other than the two specimens from the Kenaboi Mine, are the painted cast which I have mentioned above and a fragment of a much smaller circular implement made from some kind of close-grained black stone. These may, perhaps, be the specimens to which he refers. The latter, from its size, looks as if it might possibly be part of a bracelet. The larger specimens are reminiscent of a certain type of club-head from British New Guinea, but, if some specimens were made from soft stone, it seems scarcely likely that these at any rate can have been put to that use, unless used for ceremonial purposes only.

Newer acquisitions than those described above are three other quoit-like implements; one of these, of brownish, hard stone, figured on Plate XXXVII, is from Berkuning in Upper Perak. It was presented to the Perak Museum by Captain H. Berkeley, I.S.O., District Officer, Upper Perak. The other two specimens were obtained by Mr T. R. Hubback from a Pahang Malay, who told him that these objects formed part of a hoard which he discovered by chance. These are now in the Museum at Kuala Lumpur. We have also a portion of a stone "bracelet" collected from the Nyik Valley, near Kuantan, Pahang, by Mr C. W. Thomson[1].

Another curious type of implement is a water-worn stone which has had one of its faces ground almost flat and then

---

[1] Stone circlets are also known from Indo-China. *Vide Mémoires du Service Géologiques de l'Indochine*, vol. x, fascicule 1, Planches IV et V.

been deeply diagonally cross-hatched to form a diamond pattern. The F.M.S. Museums possess several examples of this kind of tool, which, judging from the analogy of the wooden bats, cross-hatched in squares, made by some Sakai groups at the present day, was probably used for a pounder in making bark cloth. Two such stones, figured here, have grooves running round them above the cross-hatched surface. These probably served for the attachment of a strong, but pliant, cane handle; in the others their shape affords a comfortable grasp for the hand[1].

Mr J. G. Watson, of the F.M.S. Forests Department has recently (1926) sent me sketches of a stone circlet of hard green stone, three of which were found, and of two sandstone cross-hatched pounders. They are said to have been discovered in association and with other stones by a Malay at Ulu Timan, Mukim Dong, Pahang, at a depth of about seven feet. The owner refuses to part with them. If the Malay's statements are correct, this would show that these two types of implement are of the same age. In 1906, a cist of granite slabs was discovered at Changkat Mentri, near the Bernam River, Perak, which contained three cornelian beads and some rough pottery. Many years afterwards, Dr R. O. Winstedt and Mr H. C. Robinson, late Director of Museums, F.M.S., did some further digging at the site and discovered a cross-hatched "bark-cloth pounder," an iron tool and some fragments of a (?) bronze vessel. A similar type of cist, containing pottery and fragments of iron, has newly been discovered at Sungkai. Dr P. van Stein Callenfels tells me that in East Java, where dolmens and cists are common, they range from a late neolithic to an iron culture.

I have already referred to two stone circlets which are said to have formed a part of a hoard of such articles. I have myself heard a story, from a Malay, of a find of stone axe heads in Upper Perak; while a Pahang Malay informant

[1] Bark-cloth beaters made of squared pieces of stone, which are grooved at the corners of their sides to take a pliant rattan handle, bent round them, are to be seen in the Batavian Museum. Their faces are ridged longitudinally or diagonally. They come from Posso, Middle Celebes.

says that tales of discoveries of large numbers of "thunder-bolts" (stone implements) are common in his country. Further confirmation of the existence of hoards is afforded by a discovery, in which I myself was concerned, of five stone implements at Tanjong Malim, all the specimens being picked up within a radius of eighteen feet. The earth in which they were found had been moved from another site and re-deposited. Further, at Batu Gajah, another hoard, two of the specimens comprising it being extremely fine, was recently brought up in a bucket of a tin dredge from a depth of fifty feet.

A very curious series of broadly lanceolate and round chipped stones, some of which are figured, have recently been obtained by Mr C. W. Thomson of Kuantan, Pahang, from a valley at Nyik, about twenty miles west from Kuantan. Other objects got from the same locality comprise a portion of a stone "bracelet"—mentioned above—two polished stone axe heads[1] and a part of another, some "hammer-stones" (of exactly similar type to some specimens discovered in a cave at Gunong Pondok, Perak), and a stone mortar cut in a water-worn block of stone, and seemingly little used, for the bowl of the specimen shows distinct marks of the (?) stone tool with which it was hollowed out. All these objects came from tailing heaps, the result of alluvial tin mining by Chinese. The alluvium from which they are derived, according to Mr Thomson, who has not seen a specimen in position, is about seven feet in depth. I deal, however, with these rough implements and pounders in the paper on cave deposits, as it has become obvious that their connection is with objects found in such situations.

Though the Malays in no way recognize stone axes for what they are, and many, at any rate, of the Sakai and Semang —like the Malays—consider them to be thunderbolts, yet there are stories current of wild tribes in the interior who are said to use stones of some kind as implements. De Morgan records legends, obtained from Sakai in the neighbourhood

---

[1] Lower neoliths (protoneoliths).

of Gunong Kerbau, of short, dark-coloured apes with curly red hair who used stone implements of some kind. They were said to clothe themselves in leaves, to live in caves, above 1500–2000 metres, to make fire and to speak a language which did not resemble that of the Malays. He also says that from Gunong Kerbau he saw the smoke of a fire, which one of his men said had been lit by these apes, and that the Sakai in order to prove their assertions, gave him two axe heads of polished stone which they said were made by the "apes who make fire."

Skeat in his *Pagan Races of the Malay Peninsula* says, "Captain J. Bradley (a sportsman travelling in the Malay Peninsula in 1876) speaks of finding in the tree-huts of the aborigines (though without giving any details which might identify either the tribe or the district) a curious instrument made of bone, apparently intended to serve as a knife, together with a sort of tomahawk formed by fixing a pointed stone upon a stick. Elsewhere the same writer speaks of finding (in the same locality) a number of sharpened stones, serving the purposes of knives[1]." The same authority—citing Vaughan Stevens—says that he (V.S.) states that a tribe of Negritos (whom he terms Orang Pangan and assigns to the district that he calls no. 2) informed him that they had formerly been in the habit of using stone weapons; and that they made, at his request, wooden models of these implements. He adds, moreover, that the Pangan recognized some stone implements which he showed them as their "old work tools." Vaughan Stevens' own editor, however, as Skeat says, very properly points out that a scrutiny of these models showed them to be identical in shape with iron tools *of the Malay type* still in use in the Peninsula. Hale mentions that a Sakai chief in Kinta told him of a race who did not know anything about iron, but used stone axes to cut down trees and Swettenham says that "it is believed that comparatively recently some at least of these tribes

---

[1] J. Bradley: *A Narrative of Travel and Sport in Burmah, Siam and the Malay Peninsula*, pp. 298, 331.

used implements of flint or slate. We thus have only one record of stone implements having been seen in the hands of aborigines of the Peninsula, the evidence of the witness in question, being, I believe, not particularly trustworthy, while rightly, or not, the whole of Vaughan Stevens' work is so discredited, and his writings, to judge by Skeat's quotations (we have not his original papers in the Museum), often so vague, that his statement that the Semang recognized stone implements as being their old work tools must— pending further affirmative evidence—be disregarded. The information given by de Morgan, Hale and Swettenham, that some of the aborigines have stories that stone implements either were, or are, used by certain of the wild tribes cannot, however, be so lightly brushed aside, and I myself have been informed by Sakai-Jakun of the Kĕrau in Pahang that the wild people of the Lompat River, a tributary of the Kĕrau still use stone tools[1]. Skeat considers that the prevalence of the tradition may be easily explained if any of these aborigines had previously used chips of flint (or other kind of stone) for knives.

A word of warning is, perhaps, necessary with regard to stories about wild tribes which are obtained either from Malays or from the tamer aborigines—the evidence of Malays with regard to the habits and customs of the aborigines is seldom to be believed, and the Sakai, too, tell wonderful stories of tribes with whom they are not in contact. Malays have sometimes informed me that aborigines, whom I was going to meet, were unable to eat salt or rice, since, if they did so, they became intoxicated. Needless to say there were no grounds for the belief, the Malays having evolved the legend in order to show their own superiority over the Sakai, a people whom they considered in so low a state that they became ill if they eat the food of a civilized people, such as they (the Malays) were.

[1] *Vide* Paper VII, *supra*.

PLATE XXXIV

COMMON TYPES OF STONE IMPLEMENTS

1. Stone adze head with chisel-like edge. From Kelantan.
2. Stone adze head from Kelantan. This type is sometimes slightly hollow-ground at the point on the "under" surface.
3. Large stone adze head from Perak.
4. Stone adze head; locality unknown. This type is sometimes evenly ground on both sides towards the point, but often grinding is more pronounced on one side than on the other, as in the present case.

PLATE XXXV

STONE IMPLEMENTS SHOWING TRACES OF WORKING

1. Large adze head from Upper Perak. The body of the implement is a water-worn stone without any sign of chipping, but one end has been ground away on either side to form a sharp edge.

2. Small unfinished adze head from Kelantan. The portion of the implement nearest the cutting edge shows chipping: the base has been ground.

3. Unfinished adze head from Kelantan. Chipping strongly marked.

PLATE XXXVI

RARE TYPES OF STONE IMPLEMENTS

1. Cast of a rare type of implement; possibly a hand axe. The proximal end (uppermost in picture) is rounded and affords an excellent grip to the hand. From Rasa, Selangor.
2. Shouldered adze head. Locality unknown.
3. Long, chisel-shaped implement from the Kenaboi Hydraulic Mine, Negri Sembilan.
4. Implement of primitive type. Nyik, Kuantan, Pahang.
5. Rare type of implement with slight groove towards proximal (upper) end. Cf. fig. 1. From Chenderiang, Perak.

PLATE XXXVII

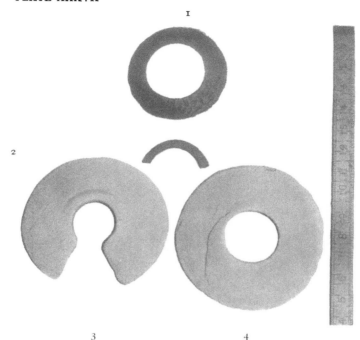

QUOIT-SHAPED OBJECTS

1. Ring of hard, black stone; flat below, bevelled above, with thick inner, and sharp outer, edge. Berkuning, Upper Perak.

2. Portion of stone "bracelet." The material is a hard, black stone.

3 and 4. Casts of two quoit-like objects found in the wash-boxes at the Kenaboi Hydraulic Mine, Negri Sembilan. The material of the originals is a curious pale, greenish-blue coloured stone of light weight. Both specimens are flattened below, but no. 4 is bevelled in the same manner as no. 1, while no. 3, though flattened above and thick at its outer edge, has a raised ring round its inner circumference above and also, to a lesser extent, below. Owing to the removal of a segment, whether by design or accident, it is not possible to say for certain, the "quoit" is incomplete.

PLATE XXXVIII

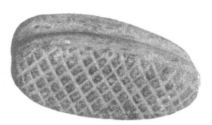

1

2

CROSS-HATCHED IMPLEMENTS
(Probably beaters for making bark cloth)

1. From Pong, Upper Perak, where it was found at a depth of 6 in. while a ditch was being cut.
2. "Bark-pounder" found 20 ft. below the surface in a mine in the Telom Valley, Pahang.

Note grooves on both specimens, presumably made for the attachment of a strong rattan loop-handle.

XXIV. CAVE EXPLORATION.

It has now become possible to trace a very considerable correspondence between the culture of the old troglodytes of the Malay Peninsula and that of some of the former inhabitants of the caves and rock shelters of Indo-China. Furthermore, a certain type of primitive implement from Sumatra, discovered by Dr P. van Callenfels of the Netherlands East Indies Archaeological Service, is related to a type from Peninsular caves, which is also found in Indo-China.

It is possible, too, to make certain general statements about the life of the cave dwellers on the evidence afforded by excavations. The following will, I think, be found to be correct.

(i) The cave dwellers lived largely by hunting, and bones, the remnants of their feasts, are found in plenty. These are usually much broken, probably having been smashed to obtain the marrow. The remains of the following animals have been encountered, the identifications having been made on teeth or horns: elephant[1], rhinoceros[1], wild cattle, deer, muntjac, serow, pig, porcupine, bamboo rat, squirrels, monkeys, soft turtles and tortoises. Fish bones are also sometimes found, but are not common. All the animal remains appear to be those of extant species.

(ii) Another article of diet was afforded by fluviatile molluscs (species of *Melania* and *Unio*) and the shells of *Melania* are found in great quantities and sometimes, when bound with lime, form a shell breccia. The topmost whorls of these spiral shells have been knocked off. The Malays still treat the molluscs in this manner before cooking them; otherwise the contents of the shells cannot be easily extracted.

(iii) The cave dwellers in many instances obtained sea shells, though often resident at considerable distances from the sea. In some cases, especially with regard to cockles and

---

[1] *Vide infra*, p. 149. The elephant's tooth may have been found in the jungle.

a kind of clam, the shells of which are common in one locality, it looks as if live shellfish had been brought from the coast for eating purposes.

(iv) Lumps of a red iron oxide, forming a ruddle, were in common use for some purpose—probably painting the body —and pieces of this material frequently show signs of having been worn down by rubbing them against some hard surface, while oval quartz pebbles, and other stones, have red staining at their ends, a clear indication that they were used for working up this paint. Such "rubbers" are sometimes considerably worn by constant use. Pieces of black haematite are also found. Grindings from these also give a red colour.

(v) Hollowed slabs—grinding slabs—and round stones—grinding stones—were also in use, and may have been for grinding up chillies, salt and other substances, but both slabs and stones are sometimes coloured with ruddle.

(vi) The working of stone, both by chipping and grinding, was known. Rough implements of a palaeolithic (Chelleo-Moustierian) type are not uncommon, but, in almost all cases, these have been found in association with implements which have been made by grinding. These, however, do not come up to the standard of finely polished neolithic culture implements, being of a very inferior type. They are generally water-worn stones, not at all, or very little, chipped, and ground on either side to form a cutting edge only.

(vii) Flakes are common and some may have been used as knives or scrapers, but there is no secondary flaking on them.

(viii) Rough cord-marked pottery, in imitation of ware made in a basket, and often with diamond-shaped reticulations, was in use at the same time as the palaeolithic type and ground stone implements, but, where deposits are deep, seems not to be found in the lower layers. Some other types of rough pottery are also to be met with, but not at considerable depths.

Before dealing with our material from a comparative point of view, let us first say something about the history of cave exploration in the country. The first record of the discovery of ancient remains in the caves of the Peninsula is of shell and bone deposits at Gunong Pondok in Perak. Mr L. Wray, a former Director of Museums, F.M.S., states that he discovered these as far back as 1880. In 1886, he carried out excavations in some rock-shelters at Gunong Cheroh, near Ipoh, in the same State. Here he found large quantities of freshwater shells, both univalves and bivalves, and noted that the topmost whorls of the univalve shells had been broken off to make the extraction of the contents easy. Some marine shells were also present. He records, too, that he excavated many land shells, and numerous bones of animals: the latter had been much broken to extract the marrow. Other discoveries were two grinding slabs ("mealing stones") and a grinding stone or muller, as well as pounding stones of hard quartz, mostly egg-shaped, and bearing signs of the use to which they had been put. In 1891, remains of two skeletons were encountered during further digging. They were those of adults and were lying on their sides with knees drawn up and close together. Wray surmised that they had not been buried, but merely left lying. The bones were very soft and much damaged, and it was not found possible to remove them except in a broken state. A hearth was noticed a short way above the skeletons. Lumps of iron ruddle and black haematite were also observed. At a later date, not specified, an implement was found, this being a large flat and elongated, water-worn stone, without any signs of chipping on it, and sharpened to an axe-edge by grinding at one end and on either side[1]. Further specimens were also discovered, these consisting of three skeletons in fragmentary condition and two more grinding slabs and a muller. Wray visited two caves at Kota Glanggi in Pahang, and saw signs of their having been recently inhabited by Sakai. He seems to have done no digging in this neighbourhood. Wray found no implements of a palaeolithic type, nor does he appear to have noticed any flakes in the deposits that he examined.

[1] The specimen is in the Perak Museum.

In 1917, I excavated parts of two small, light caves at Lenggong in Upper Perak. These yielded the first implements of palaeolithic type known from the Peninsula. Two are those figured on Plate XXXIX. The deposits were not deep, nowhere exceeding four feet, and the implements depicted on the left side of the plate lay near some broken human remains, as if purposely placed with them, at a depth of two feet. The specimen is broadly lanceolate and made from a piece of granite. A large part of the side illustrated is occupied by a central island of the original smooth and weathered, or water-worn, skin of the rock. Flakes have been removed round the edges. Trimming of a similar nature is to be observed on the other surface, though it is not so well marked. A patch in the centre of this side also appeared to be the natural skin of the stone. The other implement illustrated on Plate XXXIX is turtle-backed on the surface shown, flattish on the other. Its material is a hard and fine-grained rock, probably metamorphic, and it was found at a depth of only one foot. An island of the original skin of the pebble is left in the centre of its upper face and forms its highest part. Chipping extends from the margin to the edge of this island. The flakes removed from the under surface were much larger than those from the upper. A number of well-marked flakes were found, and several non-local stones which had evidently been brought to the caves: certain of these were chipped to some extent. One stone is very markedly worked on one side and has the rounded skin of the pebble on the other. It is a small object, but may, perhaps, be referred to the class of "Sumatran" type of implement to which I refer on p. 151[1]. No polished or ground implements were found at Lenggong. Cord-marked pottery was encountered and also some smooth ware, including what appear to be portions of two dishes with circular feet. Pottery was discovered chiefly towards the surface, and none much below a foot in depth. Other objects found were a grinding stone (muller) stained with red iron oxide, red oxide itself, haematite,

---

[1] Another implement may be classed as a "Sumatran" type scraper.

a grinding slab, shells of *Unio* and *Melania*, the latter with their topmost whorls knocked off, and numerous mammalian bones in fragmentary condition, many of them being blackened or browned by burning. No shells of marine molluscs were encountered.

In 1917, too, I did some exploration of caves at Gunong Sennyum and in the Kota Glanggi neighbourhood, both in Pahang. The cave in Gunong Sennyum, called Gua To' Long, is a long light cave which can only be reached by means of a ladder, or by swarming up the pendent roots of a *Ficus*, which grows adjacent to the cliff face. Excavations at this site yielded red iron oxide, grinding stones stained with this pigment, black haematite, shells of freshwater molluscs, cord-marked pottery, many mammalian teeth and bones, and bones of soft turtles and tortoises. Many flakes and a few implements of palaeolithic type, much like those from Gunong Pondok, illustrated on Plate XL, were also discovered. The deposits were not deep, having a maximum of only four feet. Flakes were commonest at from two to three feet; rarest towards the bottom. The palaeolithic type implements, too, were chiefly found in the middle layers. Three implements produced by grinding were discovered. Two of these, from depths of two and two-and-a-half feet, were small unchipped, water-worn stones, ground to a cutting edge at one end. The other, from a depth of two-and-a-half feet, is what appears to be the broken cutting edge of an axe of true neolithic type[1]. Both this and one of the two ruder ground implements show scratch marks at their cutting edges, due to their having been ground not long before they were thrown away. The other specimen is much worn. I again refer to the true neolith in that section of this paper in which I deal comparatively with the correspondence between the objects found in the cave deposits of Indo-China and Malaya. A human skull, which appears to be long, though cracked and, I believe, somewhat flattened laterally by pressure subsequent to death, was discovered resting on bedrock at a depth of three

---

[1] A mesoneolith (middle neolith).

feet from the surface together with some pieces of limb bones. The jaws, and other facial bones, are missing, but a small part of the upper jaw, containing a few teeth, was found separately[1]. A layer of ashes occurred above the human remains, which were very friable. Cord-marked and other rude pottery was encountered. It seems possible that some of this may have been made on the spot, since I found three lumps of worked clay which appear to have been hardened by fire. Two of these are small hillock or mound-shaped pieces, and one of them shows a finger print. The third is of irregular shape but exhibits a couple of rough markings, probably made with a wooden tool, while a piece has been pinched out of one edge, between the finger and thumb of the right hand, when the material was still soft, thus leaving an indentation. A few fragments of some fairly coarse glazed ware were found at varying depths between the surface and one foot and a half; one piece, in a different part of the cave, at two feet. One undoubted bone implement, a piece of mammalian limb bone of medium size, which had been split longitudinally, and ground down (internally) to form a point, was discovered.

At Kota Tongkat, one of the Kota Glanggi group of caves visited by Wray, I did comparatively little excavation, but obtained a fair number of flakes, cord-marked pottery, shells of *Melania*, etc. In some shelters near by I found a peculiar four-sided, grooved, sharpening stone and four pieces of fine-grained stone, one of which has a well-marked percussion bulb and has certainly been struck from a larger piece by human agency. All these are polished on one side and I believe this to be artificial. Bones were not common at Kota Tongkat.

In 1921, certain excavations were carried out at a very typical rock shelter at Gunong Pondok, Perak, by Mr W. M. Gordon, Temporary Assistant, F.M.S. Museums. These produced flakes, palaeolithic type implements (some of which

---

[1] Two or three pieces of another skull, presumably human, were also discovered. They were much stained with ruddle.

are illustrated on Plate XL), and one implement ground to a cutting edge. This was reported from a depth of eight to nine feet and with "palaeoliths" lying both above and below it. It is a piece of black stone, slightly chipped to shape and ground at one end, on either surface, to a cutting edge (Plate XL). The palaeolithic types were reported from all depths. An entirely new kind of implement was also obtained, this being represented by a series of pounding or rubbing stones of a peculiar make. These are water-worn pebbles naturally flattened laterally, but their remarkable feature is that they have been ground away in the centre on both sides (sometimes on one only) forming depressions to give a grip to the thumb and index finger. Several of these are illustrated on Plate XL. The shells of freshwater molluscs were abundant, and also sea shells (chiefly species of *Arca* and *Cyrena*), while several specimens of a *Voluta*, probably *Voluta indica*, were also found. The animal remains resembled those from other caves, but a tooth of a rhinoceros and a portion of an elephant's tooth were unearthed. Iron ruddle was common, and several pieces showed signs of having been ground down against a stone or other hard surface. Haematite was present. A quantity of round grinding stones and several slabs also came to light. The grinding stones are rounded, river-worn pebbles of varying size, many of them deeply stained with ruddle, as are also the sides of some of the pounders with grip marks. Human bones, comprising in some cases considerable parts of skeletons, nearly all much broken, were unearthed at various depths. The teeth in some of the pieces of jaws are worn down. Cord-marked and other rough pottery was also encountered. Mr Gordon's excavations, however, presented some seemingly unlikely results. In one of the pits that he dug he said that he reached bedrock at a depth of fourteen feet; in the other operations were abandoned, owing to the presence of water, at ten feet. Fragments of Chinese porcelain were reported as far down as ten feet and iron knife blades of Malay type between six and ten feet and between ten and fourteen feet; also an Annamite copper coin of a rebel chief who reigned between 1781 and 1791 at a depth of seven feet. According to Mr Gordon's showing, palaeolithic type implements lay above, as well as below, these. Further digging, of a revisory nature, has recently (1926–27) been carried out by Dr P. van Stein Callenfels and myself, a large sector between Mr Gordon's two pits being carefully opened up. I shall have occasion to refer at some length to this work later on.

In the same year (1921) as that in which Mr Gordon was occupied at Gunong Pondok, Mr G. W. Thomson of Sungei Lembing, near Kuantan, Pahang, reported to the then Director of the Raffles Museum, Singapore, the finding in the Nyik Valley, twenty miles west of Kuantan, of a palaeolithic type implement from alluvial tin workings. He subsequently obtained many more, and also pounders with grip marks exactly similar to those from Gunong Pondok. In addition, he got two stone axes—water-worn pebbles of convenient shape and size, not chipped, and ground at one end on either side to form a cutting edge. These, on the evidence from the cave deposits, I ascribe to the same culture as the palaeolithic type implements. A portion of a true neolithic-culture polished circlet, perhaps a bracelet, was also obtained from the mine tailings, as were the other specimens. Objects coming from such a source may, of course, belong to many depths, but the association of palaeolithic type implements, pounders with grip marks and implements ground to form a cutting edge only has been proved from Gunong Pondok and elsewhere.

To return now to the subject of Mr Gordon's excavations and those recently carried out by Dr P. van Stein Callenfels and myself. The site which we excavated lay in the same shelter and between the two pits that Mr Gordon dug. Our results, so far as his anomalous discoveries are concerned, do not bear out his. No iron objects were found at considerable depths, and no Chinese coins, while Chinese porcelain was only encountered quite close to the surface[1]. It is

---

[1] Except for one piece, probably carried down by burrowing animals. The soil was full of their holes.

only fair to Mr Gordon to remark that he made no pretence of being either a trained excavator or a prehistorian. He reported cord-marked and other rough pottery throughout the deposits. We traced this to a depth of only about four to five feet. It was associated with implements of palaeolithic type. Implements ground to a cutting edge only and usually not, or very little, chipped were discovered in association with those of palaeolithic type deep down in the excavation. Grip-marked pounders, haematite and ruddle were also found in connection with palaeolithic type implements from near the surface to the bottom of the deposits. A curious type of "palaeolith," of which Mr Gordon produced no specimens, was found to be common. It is made from a pebble, and has only one face chipped, the other being formed of the natural skin of the stone. The outline is usually oval, and the thickness greatest in the middle. Guided by Dr Callenfels, I have picked up implements of similar type, but much weathered and of very different material, in numbers on Soekaradja Estate, Asahan, Sumatra. The type is also known from the caves of Indo-China and one implement from Lenggong, Upper Perak, alluded to above, seems to be of the same genus. In addition to the above discoveries, several grinding slabs with deep, narrow and rounded grooves in them were found at Gunong Pondok. These are of quite a new type[1].

In dealing with this subject on its Indo-Chinese side, I have sufficiently indicated the sources of my information in the bibliography given below[2]. That for the Malay States will be found at the beginning of the section on implements of neolithic culture. As there appears to be, at any rate in some

[1] It is hoped to publish, probably in the *Journal of the F.M.S. Museums*, the full results of the work at Gunong Pondok. Two grinding slabs, hollowed on both sides, and with a small hole purposely made in the thinnest part, were also found. A specimen of a similar nature, obtained by Mr Thomson at Nyik, is now in the Raffles Museum, Singapore.

[2] *Stations Préhistoriques de Somron-Seng et de Longprao (Camboge)*, by H. Mansuy, 1902. *Mémoires du Service Géologique de l'Indochine*, vol. x, fasc. I, 1923; vol. xi, fasc. II, 1924; vol. xii, fasc. I, 1925; vol. xii, fasc. III, 1925. *Bulletin du Service Géologique de l'Indochine*, vol. vii, fasc. I, 1920; vol. vii, fasc. II, 1920; vol. xii, fasc. I, 1923; vol. xiii, fasc. III, 1924; vol. xiv, fasc. I, 1925.

respects, a close correspondence between the ruder stone culture of the Peninsula—as exemplified in caves and at Nyik—and that of certain deposits in Indo-China, I will first give a summary of the Indo-Chinese results, largely extracted from *Mémoires du Service Géologique*, vol. XII, fasc. I, and chiefly from pp. 10 and 33–36.

(1) In Tonkin a neolithic culture of which the debut is characterized by an instrument with a polished cutting edge, succeeds a palaeolithic of Chelleo-Moustierian type[1]. The immediate passage of a culture of most primitive type to a true neolithic culture with polished implements can only be explained by the arrival of ethnic elements of a more advanced culture who introduced the polishing of stone into regions where the people still employed chipped implements of the most primitive kind. No transition industry separates the palaeolithic of an ancient facies from the "lower neolithic," and polishing is observed to have been applied to the edges of some implements of primitive type which were obviously not suited to this treatment. This is evidence of the rapid, and perhaps "brutal," manner of the change. The "lower neolithic" comprises only axes of which the polishing is limited to the cutting edge. Often polishing was applied to form a cutting edge on pebbles which had undergone no, or very little, previous chipping.

(2) The caverns of Pho-Binh-Gia and of Dong-Thuoc, situated respectively on the northern and southern limits of the massif of Bac-Son, held in their deep beds stone implements of a "lower neolithic" culture, but on the other hand, of entirely different ethnical types, the one, at Pho-Binh-Gia, showing European (Cro-Magnon) affinities; the other, at Dong-Thuôc allying itself with the very dolichocephalic oceanic negroes (Melanesians). These two diverse ethnical elements co-existed in Indo-China, without any doubt, for a long series of ages, but the negroid type probably arrived first. One is inclined to attribute the introduction of polishing to the "European" element.

[1] Both types are found together.

Three prehistoric types of man are known from Indo-China.

(*a*) The Minh-Cam Skull. That of a child of nine years, which has a cephalic index of 84·96 and is of Negrito type.

(*b*) The "European" skull, *q.v. supra.*

(*c*) The "Melanesian" skull from Dong-Thuôc[1].

(3) Red paint, probably for painting the body, was used[2].

(4) Cord-marked pottery ("*au panier*") was found in the caves, but only in the upper layers. It is ascribed to an upper (later) neolithic culture. It has been found with stone implements of the finely polished type.

(5) Human bones found were, in some cases, carbonized. It is thought that this shows indifference with regard to the dead and that they were buried in shallow graves, the survivors often building their camp fires over places where bodies lay.

(6) Pounders, with grip depressions on opposite sides (sometimes only on one side) were found in a cave at Giouc-Giao in the Bac-Son massif and are said to have been common. Here they are ascribed to the "lower neolithic" but others of the same type, from a kitchen midden at Bau-Tro, Annam, were associated with objects of an upper (later) neolithic culture.

(7) The mammalian remains seem to be confined to those of extant species.

I hope that I have now set down the chief features of the discoveries of primitive-type stone cultures in the caves of Indo-China and of the conclusions drawn from them. In some places what I have extracted is almost an exact translation from the original. Let us now see how Malayan finds compare with these. The numbers in the sections below refer also to those above.

(1) The stone implements from a cave at Lenggong are of very primitive type. No trace of polished stone was found in this cave. Both implements approximating to a palaeolithic type and inferior polished implements of a neo-

---

[1] In the latest literature, just received, further racial types have been distinguished (*Mémoires*, vol. XII, fasc. III).

[2] This seems, however, to be ascribed to a true neolithic culture, but *vide Mémoires du Service Géologique*, vol. XII, fasc. I, p. 33.

lithic culture were discovered at Gunong Sennyum, Pahang, and at Gunong Pondok, Perak. At the shelter in Gunong Cheroh, Perak, excavated by Wray, only a single implement was found and that a flattened (naturally) river stone, sharpened to a cutting edge by polishing, on both sides, at one end only. Of the three inferior polished implements from Gunong Sennyum, Pahang, two were made from water-worn stones, polished at the cutting edge only, while the third consists of a broken piece of an implement—the cutting edge only. This is finely polished, and appears to belong to a true neolithic culture. At Kota Tongkat four small pieces of doubtfully polished stone were found and a few flakes. No whole implements were discovered. The rough implements from Gunong Pondok are of palaeolithic type. The polished implements found were pieces of stone not chipped, or very little, and ground, on either surface, towards the cutting edge only. I have already referred to the rough implements obtained by Mr Thomson from Nyik, Pahang, and have remarked that they resembled those of a palaeolithic culture. Two neolithic-type axes were also discovered, but these again were pebbles of convenient shape, only polished at the cutting edges. As remarked previously, Mr Thomson's specimens came from mine tailings. The portion of a stone bracelet that he found is obviously of more recent date, as are similar objects from Indo-China. It will thus, I think, be seen that we appear to have in the Malay Peninsula, a lithic culture of rude type which is much like that of Indo-China—*i.e.* a low type of neolithic culture imposed, without any transition stages, on one of primitive palaeolithic type. The presence (at Gunong Sennyum) of what appears to be a true neolithic axe-head, associated with palaeolithic type implements and ground "lower neoliths" can easily be accounted for if the palaeolithic cave dwellers acquired the art of making roughly ground implements from an invading people who had a true neolithic culture. Occasional tools of the advanced type would no doubt be acquired by barter.

(2) In Indo-China two racial elements have been distinguished in the "lower neolithic" deposits ("European" and "Melanesian"), both of which ultimately practised the same methods in the manufacture of stone implements, which one (the "European") is thought to have introduced. As the human remains from the caves of the Malay Peninsula have yet to be examined by an expert in physical anthropology, I do not care to say a great deal about this matter, but it is perhaps worth remarking that a skull from Gunong Sennyum appears to be remarkably dolichocephalic (? a "Melanesian" type). The specimen, which is the only skull in fairly good condition yet obtained, has certainly undergone lateral crushing, but, even when this is taken into consideration, still appears to be abnormally long.

(3) Red paint—probably for painting the body—was commonly used. Many grinding stones are coloured with it at the ends.

(4) Cord-marked pottery appears to be found in association with palaeolithic type (*i.e.* lower neolithic) implements, but only in the upper layers. In Indo-China it is, seemingly, associated with an upper neolithic culture only.

(5) It was noticed, both at Gunong Sennyum and at Gunong Cheroh that ashes overlay human remains.

(6) Pounders with grip depressions on opposite sides were found at Gunong Pondok, and also by Mr Thomson at Nyik. In the former case, if not in the latter as well, it is certain that they were associated with *our* "lower neolithic" culture. These pounders are identical with those of Indo-China.

(7) Animal remains found appear to be, in all cases, those of existing species, as in Indo-China.

I have now pointed out the similarities between the rude lithic cultures of Malaya and Indo-China, and I think that I have shown that they are very great. Certain deposits, found in a rock-shelter at Batu Kurau, Perak, appear to be much more modern than those dealt with above. A true neolithic axe-head was picked up on the surface before excavation was started, and another[1], some iron implements[2] and Chinese porcelain were found during excavation. No flakes and no palaeolithic type implements were discovered. The interesting deposits were only two-and-a-half feet thick and a layer of yellow sand, probably from the adjacent Kurau River, overlay them to a depth of from six inches to a foot. Shells of *Melania* were common and marine shells (*Phasaniella, Natica, Marginella* and *Cypraea*) were also present. Four of these were bored for suspension, while the only *Cypraea*, a money cowry, had its dorsal surface ground away until it also could be suspended from a cord. The second neolith was discovered at a depth of only eight inches from the surface. Rough pottery of rather Malayan type was found, but none with cord-marking. The deposits, owing to the mixture of iron objects and of Chinese porcelain with neolithic implements, afford a difficult problem. Possibly they may have been disturbed at some period by river action.

Before bringing this paper to a close I think it well to make a few remarks relative to present day users of the Peninsular rock-shelters and caves. The most recent are the Chinese, who often house themselves in such localities where they exist in populous neighbourhoods, and have even built temples in a few of the larger caves. The Negritos of Lenggong frequent the light caves to a considerable extent, and I have twice found them camped in the Gua Badak (Rhinoceros's cave). On the last occasion[3] they told me that they had been there for about six days previous to our arrival. We enlisted the men as diggers for cave exploration and the party, owing to the dust that we made, moved to another site some distance away. The Negritos frequently make charcoal drawings on the rocks, and also white pictures

---

[1] Both are of a middle neolithic culture, having an elliptical cross-section.

[2] Four blades of the kind of knife which is known to the Malays as *pisau raut*, two shoulderless adze blades of primitive type, a chopper blade of the kind which the Malays call *golok*, and two rectangular pieces, one of which is probably the lower part of an adze blade.

[3] This was in 1926, when I carried out excavations in association with Dr Callenfels. A fragment of a late neolith was found in association with cord-marked pottery as in Indo-China.

by scraping away the skin of the limestone marble rock in places where it has become discoloured. They draw animals, people and trees, mats and even such objects as motor cars and bicycles! The motor car is sometimes depicted with four wheels, because they know that it has that number. As their drawings, however, are very primitive, and they have little idea of perspective, they place the two off-side wheels of the car separate from its body, one in front and one behind. There is an excellent series of Negrito drawings in a cave near the Gua Badak.

In Pahang, some of the Kota Glanggi caves are occasionally used by the Sakai-Jakun of the Tekam River and the roof of one, the Kota Rawa, I observed to be blackened with smoke, and its floor strewn with shells of *kĕpayang* fruits. A man of this group told me that his people regularly visited the caves when these fruits were ripe, the trees which bear them being common in that neighbourhood. Wray also found signs of recent occupation in the Kota Glanggi caves, comprising sleeping-platforms, hearths, bones, molluscan shells, husks of Indian corn and shells of *kĕpayang* and other jungle fruits.

[Other objects obtained at Gunong Pondok, after this paper was in the press, comprise many Sumatran-type and other palaeoliths, Sumatran-type scrapers, lower neolithic (proto-neolithic) axe-heads, a few chipped picks, a remarkable pick made from a water-worn pebble ground to a point, and a money cowry shell of which the dorsal surface has been rubbed away so that only the lips remain. This was undoubtedly for suspension as a personal ornament. Large cowries, treated in a similar manner, have been found in Indo-China[1]. A *Pinna* shell and a canine tooth, probably from a wild dog, both bored for suspension, were also discovered. Another point worth remarking is that the human skeletons unearthed, mostly much broken, nearly all came from one corner of the excavation. They were found at considerable depths; the lowest at 5·4 metres. They were near together both with regard to their vertical and horizontal positions.]

[1] *Vide* pp. 155, 156 *supra* with reference to another cowry from Malaya.

PLATE XXXIX

STONE IMPLEMENTS FROM A CAVE AT LENGGONG, UPPER PERAK

PLATE XL

SPECIMENS FROM ROCK-SHELTER, GUNONG PONDOK, PERAK

Top row: Pounders with "grip depressions." Lengths 10·8, 12·7, 11·5 cm.
Second row: Stone implement, polished at cutting edge only, 9·4 cm.
            Piece of ruddle with abraded faces.
            Quartz pebble coloured with ruddle at ends.
Third row: Chipped stone implements of primitive type. Lengths 10·7, 10·2,
            9·3 cm.
Fourth row: Three small pieces of cord-marked pottery.

PLATE XLI

XXV. ANCIENT OBJECTS IN BRONZE, IRON AND OTHER MATERIALS

Whether or not there was a bronze age in the Peninsula appears to be somewhat doubtful, but, if there was, it seems probable, on such evidence as we have up to the present, that it was not of any considerable duration.

Certain cutting tools of bronze or copper have been discovered, but these appear to be distinctly rare. As they are all small adze heads it seems likely that either iron—a much more suitable material—was unknown or very rare at the time that they were manufactured.

Finds of bronze adze heads have been reported from the Kenaboi Mine in Negri Sembilan, where at least three such articles were taken from wash-boxes, and of single specimens from mines at Rasa in Selangor and Tanjong Malim in Perak. All the specimens are very small socketed celts and are usually broader above than towards the cutting edge. In the case of those from the Kenaboi Mine, it would appear likely that they may have been made on the spot, as a small "drop" of metal, seemingly similar to that of the adze heads, was also found in the wash-boxes.

Ancient iron tools are discovered occasionally, and these, to the Malay, are the bones of the *Mawas*, a gigantic ape-like creature which has sharp sickles sprouting from its elbows. The Perak Museum possesses casts and originals of several such iron implements including specimens from the following localities: Sengat near Ipoh, Tanjong Rambutan, and from Bengkong in the Batang Padang District of Perak; also from Klang in Selangor. The tools were presumably mining implements, and are unlike any used at the present day, nor do I remember having seen similar articles from other countries. Six of these implements are pierced for the passage of small hafts and the blades are in the same plane as the holes. Very similar examples are present from all three localities and one is, therefore, tempted to consider them contemporaneous. Two other examples, from Sengat, rather resemble one-piece iron axes with stumpy blades and comparatively long iron shafts. Associated with the examples from Klang were found an iron spear head and three large objects of bronze which appear to be bells[1]. One of these is now in the Perak Museum.

I have mentioned that an iron implement was found in connection with the dolmen grave at Changkat Mentri, a cross-hatched stone bark-cloth pounder being discovered in association with it[2], while at another dolmen grave, near Sungkai, Perak, an iron implement of the first-described type has been discovered just recently.

[1] One is figured in Winstedt's *Malaya*.
[2] Page 137.

PLATE XLII

ANCIENT SOCKETED IRON IMPLEMENTS
FROM KLANG, SELANGOR

BRONZE SOCKETED CELT
Jeher Hydraulic Mine,
Tanjong Malim, Perak.

XXVI. SOME NEOLITHIC IMPLEMENTS FROM CHONG, TRANG, PENINSULAR SIAM

Both at Chong, in the Trang-Patalung hills, and at Pata-lung, on the Inland Sea, I made enquiries as to the occurrence of ancient stone implements. In the neighbourhood of the latter place these were fruitless, but at Chong I was successful in purchasing five neoliths from the local Siamese. Of these, as will be seen from the illustration, four are of more or less ordinary type. Nos. 1 and 2 are almost regular, though slightly more ground on one cutting edge than on the other, while nos. 3 and 4 are slightly convex on one surface, indi-cating, probably, that they were hafted adze-fashion. This may also well have been the case with nos. 1 and 2.

From the Malayan point of view, the beaked implement (no. 5) is much the most interesting. Though the specimen has been very badly weathered, or water-worn, its original shape is still quite distinguishable. Implements of this peculiar type are common in the Malay States and it is interesting to trace it up into Peninsular Siam.

Mr J. B. Scrivenor, Geologist, F.M.S., has been so kind as to attempt to identify the materials of which the imple-ments are made. This is, of course, a somewhat difficult matter unless pieces are cut from the stones and made into slides, but I expressly stipulated that this must on no account be done. The results of his inspection are as follows:

No. 1. Probably a glassy lava; perhaps rhyolite.
No. 2. Probably volcanic tuff composed of fragments of rhyolite.
No. 3. Probably rhyolite.
No. 4. Probably rhyolite.
No. 5. Impossible to say without damaging the implement.

The lengths and greatest breadths of the five specimens are as follows:

1. 8·2 cm. × 4·9 cm.
2. 5·1 cm. × 3·9 cm.
3. 7·9 cm. × 4·5 cm.
4. 7·5 cm. × 4·9 cm.
5. 15·5 cm. × 5·0 cm

PLATE XLIII

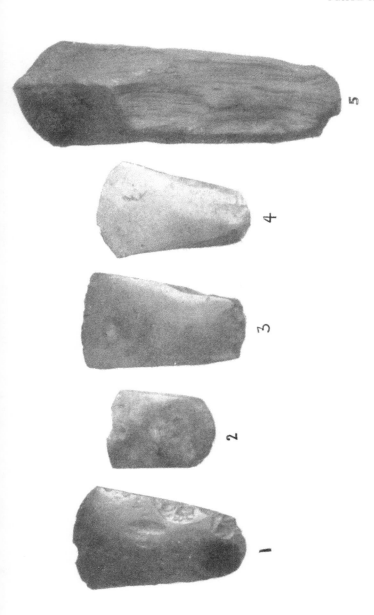

STONE IMPLEMENTS FROM CHONG, PENINSULAR SIAM

INDEX